CREATIVE IDEAS FOR TEACHING DRAMA

stages

CREATIVE IDEAS FOR TEACHING DRAMA

stages

by TALIA PURA

J. GORDON SHILLINGFORD
PUBLISHING INC

Cover design by Gallant Design Ltd.
Author photo by Image 2
Printed and bound in Canada on 100% post-consumer recycled paper.

We acknowledge the financial support of the Manitoba Arts Council, The Canada Council for the Arts and the Government of Canada through the Book Publishing Industry Development Program (BPIDP) for our publishing program.

Library and Archives Canada Cataloguing in Publication

Pura, Talia
        Stages: creative ideas for teaching drama/Talia Pura

Includes bibliographical references.
ISBN 1-896239-94-3

1. Theatre—Study and teaching. 2. Drama—Study and teaching.
I. Title.

PN1701.P87 2002   792'.071   C2002-902619-9

J. Gordon Shillingford Publishing
P.O. Box 86, RPO Corydon Avenue, Winnipeg, MB Canada R3M 3S3

For Bill, my muse.

Acknowledgements

There are a great number of people whose input and encouragement need to be acknowledged. Thanks to the inspiration from all of the students I have taught in drama classes over the years: River East, Kildonan East, Dakota, Fort Richmond and Glenlawn Collegiate in Winnipeg. Thanks also to the students of the Education Department of the University of Winnipeg, whom I trust will benefit from this book. I especially thank Sharanpal Ruprai, the student who first suggested that I put all of my teaching ideas into one volume.

Also, thanks to all of the drama coaches, directors and actors whose workshops and master classes I have attended over the years. Many of the ideas and exercises in this book are expansions and explorations of their own concepts.

A big thank you to Gord Shillingford for taking a chance on this book and allowing me to bring it to life.

Table of Contents

Introduction

During the years that I taught high school drama I collected recipe cards. Each one contained an exercise that I planned to use in my class. Some I discovered while teaching something else; some I had heard about from another drama teacher or gleaned from a workshop. Each day I would flip through the cards to find just the right exercise to round out my lesson plan or to reinforce a concept I was teaching.

When I left the public school system, I began teaching university Education students who were about to embark on careers as drama teachers. As I passed around handouts of exercises that I had used and gave students yet another page of notes to write out, a student suggested that I should just put in all in a book. So I decided to do just that. This book is an effort to file all those exercises into one portable package. They are categorized to allow you to use them to build your lesson. Just as a well-balanced, attractive meal will have a dish from more than one food group, so, too, should your lesson contain more than one type of exercise. A good drama lesson challenges students to explore themselves while building acting skills. Their minds and bodies need to warm up for the experience; they need to function as a group and trust each other in order to take risks and learn in your class. Once a climate of trust and freedom is established there is no end to the growth you will see in their confidence level and their work on the stage.

This book is packed with drama exercises that work. All have been tested on the harshest of critics, high school students. You will notice that there is a minimum of theorizing about an exercise or pontificating on its value. There are many other books where you can read all about that. Nor am I here to sell you on the value of drama in the classroom or as a tool in the rehearsal process. You bought the book because you already believe that. The purpose of this book is simply to provide you with ideas to use in a teaching environment.

It is my hope that this book will be useful to a variety of people in teaching situations:

- Student teachers collecting resource material for future use.

- Substitute teachers thrown into classroom situations, drama or otherwise.

- Teachers from other subject areas who want to add creative touches to their lessons.

- Teachers without a drama background who are asked to teach an introductory drama course.

- Professional actors and directors wanting to teach beginning acting workshops.

- Any leader of children or adults wanting to add a drama component to a course or workshop.

- Drama teachers looking for new exercises ideas.

The exercises in this book can be used in isolation to fill a spare moment of class time, or they can be used to create a drama workshop or an entire first level drama course. They are suitable for a wide range of ages and abilities and can be adapted for young children, beginning teenagers or for experienced actors.

Unless otherwise stated, it is always best to have all students working simultaneously. In beginning level drama lessons, as in recreational sports, there is a basic goal in introducing exercises and concepts:

- Keep everyone as active as possible as much of the time as possible. Structure exercises in a way that does not require students to wait for a turn in order to participate.

In the case of a drama lesson, you could add the following rules:

- Keep students working simultaneously, not only to minimize waiting time but also to avoid students feeling as if they are being watched, until they are ready to perform.

- Keep students discovering acting and interactive principles for themselves through the exercises, rather than through endless discussion and analyses after every short exercise.

Having said that, it might be useful for students to keep a journal of what they are learning in class. Five minutes at the end of each class or even every few classes should suffice in helping students to reflect on where they are going in their development.

Teaching drama is the most rewarding of teaching experiences. Not only are students developing a set of skills for the stage, they are increasing their self-confidence and ability to work cooperatively, express themselves publicly, explore their own creativity—and above all, to have fun.

warm-up
EXERCISES

Warm-up exercises are important for a number of reasons:

1. Warm-up exercises allow students to mentally shake off any events that occurred before they entered this lesson and to focus on what is to come.

2. They can act as a physical warm-up to prevent injuries from more strenuous activities.

3. Warm-up exercises can also warm the student up mentally, increasing their powers of observation and concentration, important tools in improvisation and script work.

4. Group warm-ups help to build a warm, safe classroom climate, an atmosphere conducive to students being able to take risks without fear of ridicule. Their cooperative aspect builds team spirit.

5. Many warm-up exercises teach acting skills that will become useful in improvisation and script work.

NAME GAMES

In the beginning of a new session it's important that you all learn each other's names as soon as possible. You need to use their names in order to connect with the group and they need to know their classmates' names in order to learn to trust each other and relax in the group setting.

PASS YOUR NAME

This game helps students to identify each other using alliteration, which is easier to remember than a single word.

Method: Students sit in a circle on the floor. Each student must think of an adjective beginning with the same letter as his or her name. One person says his adjective and name. (e.g., Dangerous Dan) The next player repeats this name and adds her own. (Dangerous Dan, Stupendous Sue.) Once the names have gone right around the circle, the first person must say them all. Then the group says all of them in unison.

NOTE: If the group is larger than 15, it can be divided in half. After one round, half of one group trades places with half of the other group. Then they do it again, already knowing half of the names. Finally, the whole group is brought together and the exercise is played again.

Variation #1. Instead of using an adjective, students do a physical action while saying their names. The students following them must remember the names and actions before them. Once the exercise has gone around the circle, the group performs the "name dance" all together.

Variation #2. Instead of an adjective, each student passes her name around the circle with an emotion. The person next to her repeats her name, imitating her emotion, before saying his name for the next person, using a different emotion.

THE NAME CHEER

Method: Students are asked to perform cheers that contain their names, i.e., a student spells out her name, with a word that describes her for each letter. S is for super, A is amazing, L is lovely, L is loyal, Y is just give me a yell. S-A-L-L-Y. What do you get? SALLY. What? SALLY!

Variation #1. Students write poems or raps containing their name that tell the group something about themselves.

BALLOONS

Method: A student stands in the middle of the circle and tosses the balloon in the air, saying another student's name as she does so. The student named much reach the centre and hit the balloon into the air again, saying another student's name before it touches the ground.

BALLS

Method: The group forms a circle. A student begins by passing a ball to another student, calling him by name. The student who catches it does the same to another student in the circle, and so on, until each student has caught the ball several times.

INTERVIEWS

Method: In pairs, students interview each other. They find out such details as their partner's name, age, favourite music, family background. Then the group sits in a circle and the pairs introduce each other to the group.

SELL YOUR NAME

Method: For a group with some previous exposure to drama, students are given the homework of writing commercials for their names. In the next class they perform the commercials, which highlight their names in some way. The objective is to sell the group on why theirs is the greatest name.

COMPLIMENT

As an exercise to build a positive classroom climate, this exercise can be used once students already know each other a little. It can give them a really positive boost to hear what others think about aspect of their personality.

Method: Students write their names on their own pieces of paper. All papers are passed around the circle, with each person writing something they like about the person whose name appears at the top. Finally it will again reach the owner of the paper.

Variation #1. Instead of a little piece of paper, each person puts a poster-sized piece of paper on the walls of the classroom. Each student is given a felt marker and 15 minutes in which to write on other people's posters.

NECKLACE

This exercise provides students with an opportunity to get to know their fellow students in a very positive one-on-one way.

Method: Each student is given a length of coloured yarn with many short pieces of the same colour tied to it. This long piece of yarn is tied into a loop and worn around the student's neck. The group is given a length of time in which to approach each other and trade pieces of yarn, until everyone is wearing a multi-coloured "necklace."

SAY MY NAME

This is a rather high-pressure but fun game, which quickly determines if all the students know each others' names.

Method: Students stand in a circle. One student stands in the centre. He walks towards one of the students on the outside of the circle. As soon as eye contact is made, the student on the outside makes eye contact with someone else on the outside of the circle. That person must say the name of the person that the centre student is headed for before the centre student tags her. If she gets tagged, the student who didn't call her name goes into the centre of the circle. Example: Bill is in the centre. Bill walks towards Jane, who looks at Don. Don yells, "Jane," before Bill can tag her. Bill approaches Julie. Julie looks at Ted, who can't think of her name fast enough. Bill tags her. Ted goes into the centre of the circle.

NAME TAG—see LOW ORGANIZED GAMES

ROAD TRIP—see STUPID TRICKS

KEEP THE BEAT—see CONCENTRATION EXERCISES

GROUP WARM-UPS

SPREAD OUT

The following exercises require enough open floor space to allow students to move freely.

ATOM 2

This popular game is great for getting students used to physical contact with each other in a natural, non-threatening way. It's a good icebreaker that they'll love to play over and over.

Method: Leader explains that an atom is a molecular structure. For the purposes of this exercise it can be made up of any number of segments. The leader calls out "Atom" and a number. Students must form a group containing that number. Atom 1 would be each student moving about the room on his own. Atom 2 means that he needs to find one partner. Atom 3 requires him to find two partners. When in a group or partnership, students can stand still. After playing this games several times, when students are comfortable with each other, it may be played with an elimination round. Anyone not in a group of the appropriate size is out of the game. It runs until only two people are left.

Modification for young children: Have them form elephant trunks with their arms and walk around while the leader says, "Elephants, giraffes, going out for lunch, I want to see (three) in a bunch." Play without elimination. Children just wait for the next number called if they don't find a group.

SHARK-INFESTED WATERS

This exercise focuses on cooperation and teamwork.

Method: A large picnic blanket is spread out on the floor, representing a life raft. Students are asked to pretend to swim around the raft, while the leader narrates the action, commenting on the lovely sunny weather and clear water. Without warning, she shouts "SHARK," which is the command to get onto the life raft. Once the leader gives the all-clear sign, having determined that the shark has left the area, the students can again swim about. The blanket is folded after each shark slighting, making it more difficult for everyone to fit onto the raft.

NOTE: This can also be played with sheets of newspaper, or gym mats. They could be scattered around in the playing area as small life rafts.

SHIP TO SHORE

Method: The room is treated as if it were a ship, with the centre of the room named the CROW'S NEST, and the walls named the:

BOW (front of the ship)   STERN (Back)
PORT (left side)   STARBOARD (right side)

Various actions and postures of the students represent objects and activities associated with the ship:

HIT THE DECK (students lie face down on the floor).

MAN OVERBOARD (students find a partner, with each holding a foot of a third student, in a "wheelbarrow" position).

SUBMARINE (students lie on their backs, with one leg held up towards the ceiling).

DIVE-BOMBERS (student run with out stretched arms making airplane noises).

HELICOPTER LANDING (students hold a partner by both hands and circle each other).

OFFICER ABOARD (students line up at attention and hold a salute).

CAPTAIN'S DAUGHTER (A student sinks to one knee and another student sits on his or her knee).

The leader calls out a location to run to or a command, with students responding as quickly as possible before the next command is given.

Variation #1. The rule may be set that the last student to respond to a command must perform five push-ups.

NEWSPAPER STORM

This exercise focuses on cooperation and teamwork.

Method: An imaginary line is drawn down the centre of the floor. The group is divided into two teams, each team covering their half of the playing area with single sheets of newspaper. On the command to begin, each team attempts to throw all of their newspapers onto the opposite team's side of the playing area. Play continues until one team is successful (almost impossible) or time is called.

TAKE THE MOVE

A fast-paced physical warm-up, this exercise also encourages observation of the student's direct environment.

Method: Students spread out and move about the playing area, performing a simple repetitive movement. At the direction of the leader, they copy someone else's movement, abandoning their own. If at any time they notice someone copying their movements, they must switch to someone else's. The result is ever-changing movement patterns, where no two students are alike for more than a few seconds.

HELLO

The focus here is on building group dynamics and taking risks.

Method: All students mingle throughout the playing area. Whenever they encounter another student they are to look them in the eye and say hello. After a few minutes, new directions are added:

- Whisper hello in your loudest stage whisper.

- Say hello non-verbally, using your hand, now just your eyes, etc.

- Sing hello and begin a conversation in your biggest operatic singing voice.

- Say hello as different characters: An Old West cowboy
                                        An alien from outer space
                                        A big Hollywood star
                                        A very young child
                                        A very old person
                                        A nursery school teacher
                                        A personal trainer

WINK OF DEATH

Observation is the focus of this exercise.

Method: Students stand in a circle, facing out of the circle, their eyes closed. The leader walks around the inside of the circle and taps one student on the shoulder. This student now has the powerful "wink of death." Students mingle around the playing area, making eye contact with everyone else. If they get winked at, they must count to five (to make "who done it" less obvious), die a very dramatic death, and drag themselves out of the playing area. If a player (who is still alive) thinks she knows who is doing the winking, she takes a guess. If she is right, the round is over. If wrong, she too is out of the game.

NOTE: If the group is large, two murderers may be chosen. If one winks at the other, there is only one murderer left. If both wink at each other, the round is over.

Variation #1. Instead of a wink, a handshake may be used. All students shake hands with each other during play. The murderer will tickle the victim's palm with her index finger.

Variation #2. A fun, but slower, way of choosing the murderer is to have all students pick a card from a deck, with a certain card indicating who the murderer will be.

Variation #3. Instead of mingling, the exercise can be played sitting in a circle. It is more difficult to be sneaky in this formation.

Variation #4. This exercise can be played with the lights dimmed. Only two night watchmen look for the murderer within the group. He is tapping players on the head instead of winking. They try to find out who is doing it before all the other players are dead.

THE COIN

Method: A coin is passed from person to person as the students mingle about the room. One person has been chosen to watch and try to discover who has the coin. When a player is touched on the arm by the searcher, she must open both of her hands. When the coin is found, that player is the next searcher.

PASS THE MESSAGE

The objective of this exercise is to listen carefully and try to keep the message in its original form as it is passed around. It is a more elaborate version of the game "Telephone."

Method: Divide the group into smaller groups of five. Each group numbers their team members from one to five. Have all the number ones go to one area of the room, all number twos to another, and so on. An obstacle course is set up between stations as objects and space allow. Number ones are all given the same message to read, but they cannot keep the paper. After reading it, they go through the obstacle course to reach station two and whisper the message to their number two players. Number two makes his way to number three and so one until number five hears the message and writes it down. The team that keeps the message closest to the original wins.

Sample messages:

> ENEMY LINES— "Reconnaissance mission, ABLE CHARLIE VICTOR 3, reports 4 Tiger tanks and back-up platoon on southeast corner of hill 625."

> POLICE RAID— "The cops are onto us. Stash the loot in the back of the truck, pick up Joe and Bob and meet me at 450 Wilson Avenue. We have to make a new plan."

> SPIES IN THE CLUB— "Glen just walked in. If he sees me my cover is blown. You keep dancing, try to distract him. I'll sneak out the back way."

YOU'RE FAMOUS

Method: Students form groups of six or eight. One player from each group leaves the room while the rest decide on a famous person. When the players return, their groups treat them as the famous people they chose. Once the players decide who they are supposed to be they play along and become the famous person. The exercise is repeated until each group member has had an opportunity to play.

Variation #1. Instead of a famous person, the group treats the player as a certain animal.

Variation #2. Instead of a famous person, the group decides on a special physical feature for the player.

Sample features: an extra leg, a very long nose, eyes in the back of the head, a tail, no thumbs, fangs for teeth, no ears, huge clown feet.

MAGIC WORD

Method: One student leaves the room and the group decides on a "magic" word. The person comes back into the group and can ask anyone a question about any subject. The answer given must contain the magic word. After several questions, the person can guess what the magic word is. He gets three guesses before another person leaves the room.

Variation #1. Instead of using a certain word, there is a common gesture that everyone will use in the answer; e.g., always scratch an itch during your answer. Always cross, or uncross your legs. Always look to your left before giving an answer. Always give a short laugh in your answer. Always fold your arms during your answer. Always touch your hair before giving an answer.

Variation #2. Instead of using a certain word, there is a certain idea that everyone will incorporate into the answer; e.g., always mention a food in your answer. Always mention the weather. Always ask a question during your answer. Always pretend to misunderstand the question at first. Always use a number in your answer. Always name a colour.

NOTE: The trick, of course, is to be subtle in the inclusion of the magic word or deed. This requires that answers are not too short. In this respect, the exercise is challenging for all the participants, not just for the player trying to discover the answer.

SHOE MOUNTAIN

This is an observation exercise using the sense of touch. It is suitable for any age, at any stage in the lessons. It is best with a group of 10 to 15 students. If the group is larger, split it in half. It's as much fun to watch as it is to play.

Method: Students take off their shoes and place them in a pile in the middle of the playing area. They move to the periphery of the playing area and close their eyes. The leader mixes up the shoes in the pile. Students must try to find and put on their own shoes while keeping their eyes closed.

     stages • CREATIVE IDEAS FOR TEACHING DRAMA

BEANBAG TOSS

These exercises range from easy for very young children to very difficult for young adults. These exercises are used to improve hand-eye coordination and build team cooperation.

Method: Give each student a beanbag. Encourage them to explore as many ways of tossing and catching it themselves as they can.

Variations #1. In pairs: toss one bag back and forth.

■ Toss and turn before catching.

■ Toss two bags at the same time. Try variations to make it more challenging; use alternate hands, toss and turn around before catching, etc.

Variation #2. In groups of four: Toss around the circle, beginning with one bag and working up to four.

■ Toss across circle first, and then toss to the right. Repeat pattern.

■ Toss across, toss right, toss across, toss left. Repeat pattern.

Variation #3. In groups of six: starting with one beanbag, toss to anyone in the group, who tosses to another, until everyone has touched it, in random order. Repeat pattern, adding beanbags, until all six are in play.

POLE TOSS

The focus of these exercises is on hand-eye coordination, communication and concentration.

These exercises are more advanced than those for beanbags and are recommended for older students and adults. Each participant needs a pole (a one-inch dowel about three feet long). They can be easily purchased at a hardware or lumber store.

Method: Begin with the students in one large circle. The pole is carefully tossed vertically from one student to the next. Eye contact is made before the toss. Concentration is enhanced by silence. A rhythm may be set for the exercise by playing music. Soft instrumental music will produce a different feel to the exercise than bongo drums. Experiment.

Variation #1. When the students are comfortable with the tossing and catching, add a second pole, and then a third and fourth.

Variation #2. Add the second pole going in the opposite direction, so that a student will have to deal with two poles at the cross-over point. When they are ready, add a third and a fourth pole.

Variation #3. When they are ready, break the group into two and repeat the exercise. A smaller group means more contacts as the poles make their way around the circle.

Variation #4. At any point during the previous variations, students could be encouraged to play with the pole before passing it on, moving in time to the music.

Variation #5. More advanced work can be done by placing a student in the centre of the smaller circles, with two poles to control. The student passes them one at a time to various students on the outside of the circle, who pass them back to the centre. Eye contact must always be made before a toss. One pole is tossed, the other pole is tossed, the first pole is caught, the second pole is caught as the first one is tossed again, and so on. The students should continue until they achieve a comfortable flow and significant degree of control over the poles, before another student is given a turn in the centre.

Variation #6. Pole work can also be practiced between two people, first with one pole, and then with two. Eye contact and concentration are important. Again, music can be used to emphasize the style of the movement, rather than just the coordination aspect.

SOUND FAMILIES

This sensory exercise focuses on listening.

Method: Divide students into groups of five or six. After they have chosen a "family sound," something that they vocalize or make with their bodies (such as hand-slapping on thighs), have students scatter about the space, then close their eyes and begin to make their sound. They must try to find their other group members by identifying their sound from among all the other sounds in the room made by other groups.

Variation #1. Instead of a vocal sound, students decide on a family rhythm made with a series of handclaps and finger-snaps.

BIRTHDAY LINE-UP

This exercise focuses on non-verbal communication.

Method: Ask students to line up according to their birthdates, with January being at one end of the line and December at the other. They must not speak at all while forming the line.

THE WRAP

Method: Students form one straight line, holding hands. The person at the end becomes the centre of the coil, staying in one place while the rest of the line wraps around her in a circle, until everyone is wound up in a tight coil. The last person to stop then starts the action to unwind the coil.

Variation #1. The centre student can stand still as the student at the other end begins to jog in an ever-tightening circle around him until everyone is in a tight coil.

Variation #2. Instead of the last student beginning the unwrapping process, the student in the centre can duck under the arms of the entire coil and lead everyone out, beginning from the inside.

FOLLOW THE LEADER

Method: The leader moves about the space with a repetitive sound and movement. As the leader changes the sound and movement there is a wave effect, with each student changing to match the player in front of him.

RED

Method: On the command from the leader, everyone must touch a red object or a red part of the room. The colour can't be on a person. The leader keeps calling out colours for the group to find and touch. A penalty, such as doing five push-ups, could be set for the last person to reach a particular colour. Shapes can also be called, as in, "touch something that is square (or round, or diamond shaped)." Or objects made of specific materials could be called, such as wood, glass or metal.

WHAT IS IT?

This game helps warm up the student's mind, intellectually and imaginatively.

Method: Students walk around the room, naming every inanimate object they see, pointing to it and naming it. After a few moments, at the teacher's command, they continue pointing to objects, naming them anything BUT what they really are.

NOTE: It is important to stress before the exercise begins that they are to point ONLY to the INANIMATE objects in the space (wall, chair, floor, window, etc.). If they also point at other people, they can get quite nasty in the second part, in an attempt to be humorous.

AS ONE VOICE

This exercise highlights the need to listen and observe one's partners. This is a useful skill in improvisation.

Method: Students form groups of five or six members. Group members link arms and function as one person. The leader asks each small group in turn to answer a simple question. The small group attempts to sense what their group will say in response and answers the question spontaneously, with everyone speaking together as one voice.

CIRCLE EXERCISES

The following exercises are all played in a circle formation. While it works well to have one or two short exercises follow each other in the same group formation, it is best to keep the lesson interesting by changing formations often. A circle warm-up could be followed by one in which the students scatter and are very active, followed by a partners warm-up, followed by small group work, and so on.

NAME THE OBJECTS

Method: Students are seated in a circle. A collection of ordinary household objects is placed in the centre of the circle. Students are given several seconds to view the objects before they are covered with a towel or blanket. The students then make a list of everything they remember seeing.

Variation #1. Instead of covering the objects, students close their eyes while one object is removed. Each student tries to be the first to identify the object that is missing.

PASS THE BALLOON

Method: Students stand in a fairly tight circle with their shoes off. A balloon is passed around the circle from person to person using only their feet. Students try not to allow the balloon to touch the floor.

JUMP UP

This exercise requires students to work cooperatively.

Method: Students put their arms around each other's shoulders. On the signal from the leader, who stands in the centre of the circle, everyone jumps a foot off the floor, all trying to jump at the same time.

Variation #1. Instead of trying to jump together, each person jumps right after the person beside him or her, creating a wave effect.

SEW IT UP

This exercise requires a great deal of cooperation. It can be done by two groups at the same time, each making their own circle, as a relay race to see which group can accomplish the task the fastest.

Method: A long sturdy length of string is tied to a short, notched dowel or other object that will not allow the string to slip off. Together they become a needle and thread. On the command to begin, the first member of each team threads the object through his clothing, from top to bottom (e.g., through the neck of his shirt, down the waist of his pants and out the end of one pant leg). He unwinds the string as he does so, leaving it behind in his clothing as he passes it to the next player, who will thread the needle through her clothing, starting at the bottom and working her way up to the neck, unwinding the string as she goes. When the last person is connected, he begins to reverse the action, pulling the needle back through his clothing, winding up the string as he does so. The whole group remains fairly involved throughout the exercise, taking up or letting out the slack in the string as needed, keeping it from becoming knotted.

SPIDER WEB

This exercise focuses on verbal communication and teamwork.

Method: Students close their eyes and reach their hands into the centre of the circle, grabbing the hands of two other players. They then open their eyes and try to untangle the web without dropping hands, trying to get back into a single circle again.

Variation #1. Students hold hands with the people next to them in the circle, and then tangle themselves up by stepping over other people's clasped hands and crawling between legs. Once a complicated web has been created, they try to untangle it and get back to the original circle, holding hands throughout the exercise.

HEADLIGHTS

Method: Students stand in a circle. One student goes to the centre. He may point at any student on the outside and call out, "head-lights." Immediately, the student he points at holds out her arms as if she were driving, holding on to the steering wheel, while the students on each side of her circle their eyes with their hands, as if they were binoculars, representing the headlights. If a student doesn't respond with the correct posture in five seconds, he goes to the centre of the circle.

Variation #1. To make this exercise more challenging, more commands may be added, so that students don't know what is coming before it is called.

Sample commands:

- Three Monkeys—students form the "see no evil, hear no evil, speak no evil" monkey tableau.

- The Flag—the middle person rounds her arms above her head to represent the Maple Leaf. The outside students raise their arms to represent the white strips.

- Rock Star—the centre student holds a microphone, the student on the right plays guitar and the student on the left plays drums.

- Elephant—the centre student forms a trunk, while the students on each side form ears.

ZIP ZAP BOING

Method: The leader begins the exercise by pointing to the student on her right and saying, ZIP. The play continues from there. If a student says, "zip," she points to the person next to her in the circle, on her right. If she says, "zap," she points back to the person on her left. If she says, "boing," she points with both hands to a student across the circle from her. The receiving student may either ZIP the person on his right, ZAP it to his left, or BOING it to someone else across the circle.

ELECTRIC CURRENT

Method: Students cross their forearms and hold hands with the person next to them. The leader begins by squeezing the hand of the person on her right, with her left hand. He squeezes the hand of the person on his right, and so the current makes its way around the circle as quickly as possible.

PENALTIES

Method: Divide the group into circles of no more than ten students each. Each circle receives a ball to pass around. On the command from the leader (or the blow of a whistle, clap of a tambourine) the ball starts its way around each circle. On the next command, whoever is caught holding the ball receives their first penalty. Now, every time they are passed the ball, they must squat on the floor and stand back up before passing it along. Play continues with many commands to start and stop, until each group member has been caught at least twice. The penalties increase each time a student is caught.

Sample penalties:

> First penalty—squat down, stand up, pass the ball.
> Second penalty—squat down, stand up, pass the ball, bark like a dog, turn around.
> Third penalty—squat down, stand up, pass the ball, bark, turn around, jump, quack like a duck.

PASS THE POSTURE

This exercise focuses on spontaneity, but is also very useful in developing group energy.

Method: One player makes an interesting face, accompanied by a large movement and vocalization (but no words). The person next to him copies it exactly and passes it on to the next person.

Variation #1. The person receives the posture passed to him, but allows it to become exaggerated before passing it on. The posture will grow as it makes its way around the circle. This exercise also illustrates the first rule of physical comedy, which is to imitate and exaggerate.

Variation #2. The person receives and imitates the posture she is passed, but allows it to transform into her own sound and posture before passing it on.

Variation #3. The player gives a large physical reaction to the posture given. Then she creates a new one, which she passes on the next person, who reacts to it before creating a new one.

PASS THE RHYTHM

The focus here is on concentration and risk-taking.

Method: One student in the circle creates a rhythm by making a repetitive sound and movement. She takes this into the centre of the circle, crossing over to another student, whom she teaches the rhythm. The new student imitates the sound and movement, takes it into the centre and allows it to transform into a new rhythm, which he then teaches to someone else, and the process continues.

Variation #1. The first student teaches her sound and movement to another student and they both continue to perform it, leaving the circle as they do so. Another student is selected to teach another sound and movement to a student across from him. They move out of the circle with it. Eventually, all students are paired up and performing a sound and movement. They can then be instructed to retain the same sound and movement, but vary the intent or speed that they give it.

Sample intents: hostile, shy, fearful, aggressive, jealous, curious.

Sample speeds: Slow, fast, freeze-frame, slow motion.

TRANSFORMATION

This exercise focuses on developing the student's imagination and spontaneity.

Method: The group stands in a circle. An object to passed from player to player, with each person using the object as anything other than what is actually is; e.g., a paintbrush becomes a microphone, a spatula to flip a pancake, or a telephone. The object must be used, but no verbal explanation given—the way in which it is used should make its identity clear.

Other objects suitable for transformation: a pole or yardstick, a ping-pong paddle, a scarf or towel, a blackboard eraser, a pop bottle.

JOIN IN WITH A WHO

This exercise focuses on observation, concentration and pantomime skills.

Method: One player begins an activity as a specific character in a specific location; for example, a cashier in a supermarket. Other characters join the scene, becoming the customer, the manager, shelf stocker, and so on.

Sample characters and locations:

> Judge in a court
> Pet owner in a vet's waiting room
> Pilot in a plane
> Teacher in a classroom
> Tour guide in a museum
> Lifeguard at a pool
> Aerobics instructor in a gym

The first player may begin with his or her own idea or by picking a character and location from a deck of cards held by the leader.

GO WITH THE FLOW

Spontaneity, concentration, risk-taking and group communication are all brought into play with this exercise.

Method: One person begins a repetitive sound and movement (on the spot). This is followed by the rest of the group and continued until it evolves into something else. Anyone can initiate a subtle change at any time. Everyone must be sensitive to the possibility of change and go with the flow.

Variation #1. Once the group is more advanced in their improv skills, the flow can develop into scene work, with a scene naturally flowing out of a certain movement. This movement would remind one player of a character and he would begin a scene by speaking and reacting as that character. The rest of the group would respond to the character by taking on roles that fit the scene. The scene would then flow into another movement, which would flow into another scene. This is best done in small groups of four to eight students.

MIME EXERCISES

Technically, the word mime refers to the vocabulary of Corporal Mime, where there is a specific way of showing various objects and activities. In a beginning drama class without a mime skills unit, it is nevertheless useful to include exercises that allow the students to discover some basic mime for themselves, such as the pantomime (story without words) exercises in other chapters, and the following exercises which focus on "object permanence." Once an object has been established for the audience, its shape, height, weight and size should not change. A lid removed from a jar should not disappear into thin air. The audience should see what happened to it. An object placed in a certain spot should not reappear in another.

TOSS THE BALL

This exercise allows students to develop their mime skills, as they represent the different kinds of balls, but they must also concentrate, so they can tell when the ball is being tossed to them.

Method: Students toss an imaginary ball back and forth to various students in the circle. The leader changes the type of ball being mimed at frequent intervals. The students must then catch and toss the ball in a manner appropriate to its size and weight.

Sample balls: Basketball, beach ball, shot put, ping-pong ball, tennis ball, medicine ball, balloon, etc.

JOIN IN WITH A WHAT

This exercise focuses on observation, concentration and pantomime skills.

Method: One player begins the exercise by miming an action with an imaginary tool, such as painting a fence. The rest of the group will join in with their own interpretation of the activity, with their own imaginary objects, once they have figured out what she is doing.

Sample objects and activities:

> Digging a hole
> Sweeping a floor
> Planting a flower
> Washing a car
> Brushing a horse

The first player may begin with his or her own idea or by picking an object from a card in a deck held by the leader.

BOARD GAME

Method: Students sit on the floor in groups of four or five. In the centre of their circle is an imaginary board game of their choice. The objective of the exercise is to make the objects used in the playing of the game seem as real as possible. They must remember where their players are on the board from one turn to another, and keep track of objects such as dice or cards that might be used in their game.

IN THE MIRROR

Method: In pairs, students take turns getting ready in the morning by performing whatever ritual is common to them in the bathroom mirror. Their partners watch to see what they are doing and what objects they use. After one minute they report back to their partners what they saw, asking questions about any objects that were not clear, or that disappeared after use. The exercise is repeated with reversed roles.

Variation #1. Any other activity involving small objects could also be used, such as doing math homework with a calculator, pencil, eraser, book and paper; fixing a snack or baking cookies.

CIRCLE MIME

Method: Each student performs a short pantomime involving any mimed object, timed at fifteen seconds. They must fill the entire fifteen seconds. The pantomimes are not related to each other, but are events unto themselves. The second time around the circle, each pantomime is timed at ten seconds, and then five. In the next round they are once again timed at fifteen seconds.

THE RESTAURANT

Method: Students sit on real chairs around small imaginary tables. Some students act as waiters, as the whole group enacts a scene in a restaurant, where menus are studied, orders taken and delivered and food eaten. The exercise may be repeated with different groupings, allowing some patrons to become waiters and the waiters to sit at a table.

MAKING DINNER

Method: Students are divided into pairs. One student from each pair performs simultaneously as a group while the other students watch. Each student is personally responsible for observing the performance of his own partner. Performers are instructed to mime the making of a simple meal or snack. They must establish, in mime, the height of the table they are working on by always picking up and placing mimed objects at the same height. The size, weight and shape of the objects they use should remain constant. They must also try to clearly show what it is they are making. After the leader has called "time," observers are asked to identify what they believed their partners were making. The exercise is repeated with the other partner performing the mime.

INFOMERCIAL

Method: Students perform for the group one at a time or in pairs, demonstrating a product they would like to sell. The object for sale should be fairly complicated, allowing for much mimed manipulations or parts that can be added or removed from the main object.

Variation #1. The performance could be done with speech, or in "gibberish" made up language sounds that allow the student to speak without worrying what to say. The intent comes through their intonation and the clarity of their actions.

BUILD A ROOM

Method: A student enters the middle of the circle and mimes opening a door. The next student imitates opening the door and adds another element, turning on a light, perhaps. The third student repeats the first two elements and adds another: hanging up a jacket, for example. Each student adds one element to the room by interacting with some object in it. Once everyone has added something, the mimed room can become the setting for improvs. Two or three students at a time use the room to create a scene, with the rest of the group watching to make sure that the students keep the room intact and use previously established objects.

Variation #1. As the students begin to use the created room in a scene, they could be given a point for each time they use an object in the room within the context of the scene.

LOW ORGANIZED GAMES

There are many traditional childhood games that are very good for the beginning drama group, providing students with a framework in which to develop team spirit and energy. They break the ice for a new group in a non-threatening way; they also remind students that they are never too old to play. Drama requires them to keep in touch with the child they were, to remain open to just enjoying the act of letting go and having fun.

BREAK THROUGH (British Bulldog)

Method: Divided into two teams, the students line up holding hands, facing each other. The teams take turns sending one player across to the other line with the player attempting to break through the opponent's line. If she is held off, she joins the other team. If she succeeds in forcing the hands apart and breaking through the line, she returns to her own team.

BLOB TAG

Method: The students scatter throughout the room and everyone closes their eyes. Slowly, they reach out for other people. Once they touch someone else, they hang on to each other and look for others. The game continues until everyone is in one large blob.

BLIND TAG

Method: Students scatter throughout the playing area and close their eyes. Slowly, they move around the area, trying to sense where the other students are, but trying not to touch anyone. If they do, both players open their eyes and stay on the spot. Play continues until all players are standing with their eyes open.

BALL TAG

One way of finding out who's "It," is to have students stand in a circle with their feet shoulder-width apart, touching the feet of the students beside them. The ball is tossed into the circle and will roll between someone's legs. That student is 'It'.

Method: The leader holds a soft ball (large sponge or plastic children's ball). The student to be 'It' is chosen. The ball is thrown into the room and everyone is free to scatter until the person who is "It" picks up the ball, at which point she yells, "freeze," and everyone must stop. "It" throws the ball at another student (below the waist). If the person is struck, he is "It." All students scatter whenever the ball is free, and must freeze whenever it is in the hands of "It," who must also remain on the spot in which the ball was picked up and throw it from there.

Variation #1. When a player is hit, they become "It" along with everyone else who has been hit, until no one is left. Everyone must still freeze when the ball is in someone's hands, but they may pass it between themselves to get nearer to their prey.

FREEZE TAG

Method: One student is "It" and chases the rest of the group. When someone is tagged, they freeze with their arms out to their sides. In order to be freed, another player must run under their outstretched arm.

NAME TAG

Method: One student is "It" and chases the rest of the group. Whoever he is chasing calls out the name of another student before being tagged. The name that was called becomes "It" until another name is called. If a player is tagged before naming another student, then he is "It."

CAT AND MOUSE

Method: Students pair up and then form a circle, two deep, with partners standing one behind the other. One pair is not in the circle. They become the cat and the mouse, the cat chasing the mouse in and out of the circle. If the mouse is caught, they immediately change roles. The mouse stops being the mouse by standing in front of a pair of students. The back player of that pair now becomes the mouse and must immediately run from the cat.

FRUIT BASKET UPSET

This old classic has been the favourite of many a class.

Method: Students sit in a circle on chairs. Four different names of fruit are chosen and everyone becomes one of them by counting off around the circle; i.e., apple, orange, banana, pear, apple, orange, banana, etc. One chair is taken away and that student stands in the centre of the circle and calls out one of the fruits.

All students of that fruit must stand up and find another chair to sit in. The centre student also finds an empty chair, so there will always be one student left without a chair who goes to the centre of the circle. The student may call out one, two or three groups of fruit to change at the same time. She may also call "fruit basket upset," in which case all students must change. Stating the rule that students must find a chair at least two seats away from their original chairs prevents all students from simply moving one seat to the right on every upset.

RELAY RACES

There are so many relay races to do—the only limitations are space and imagination. Using relay races in a drama setting fosters teamwork and builds group energy.

Sample races:

Vary the way students move across the floor—crab crawl, backwards, hopping on one foot, etc.

Vary what they have to do once they reach the end of the playing area before coming back to their team—put on an article of clothing, eat something, stack or unstack something, etc.

PARTNER WARM-UPS

Working with a partner is an important part of a student's development, as a person and as an actor. On stage, it's always important to communicate with the other actors and to understand your character's relationship with the other characters. This requires focus and concentration. It's important to listen in order to communicate. For the student's personal development, partner work is the first step in getting along with peers. Having students work with everyone else in the class fosters a strong team effort in all class work. Never allow students to only work with one or two friends with whom they are already comfortable. This does nothing to encourage a strong group focus or create an environment in which it is safe and desirable to take risks. Without such an environment, no progress will be made.

There are many ways to insure that partners will be rotated regularly. In the space of an hour-long class, each person will likely go through at least five different partners in pair warm-ups and improvisation exercises.

Ways of pairing students:

1. Play a game of Atom. Stop the game after Atom 2 has been called.

2. Count off students while in a circle, counting up to half the groups' total number, twice. Then have the students find their matching numbers.

3. Tell students to turn to the person beside them and say, "You are my partner."

4. Have student walk to the other side of the room and find someone they haven't worked with in days.

5. After another exercise involving pairs, in which the pairs were labeled "person A" and "person B," ask all the Bs to sit down and all the As to find a new B.

6. Play one of the following warm-up exercises, which will result in pairs finding their "match."

MATCH UP

Method: Seat students in a circle, placing a label on each of their backs with a loop of tape. Instruct students to stand and approach other students, describing in pantomime what they read on the other's back. No words can be spoken. When they have someone mime back the same thing to them as they are giving, they know they have found their partners.

Sample labels: rose, garlic, newspaper, Christmas tree, moon, telephone, banana, sandwich, skateboard, stopwatch, boa constrictor, puppy, etc.

NOTE: Have one group of three labels, in case the group has an uneven number of participants.

PICK A CARD

Method: Seat students in a circle, inviting each to pick a card from a deck. The leader moves once around the circle to have students pick a card, and then moves around it once more to collect the cards. She instructs students to move around the room, interacting with all the other students.

Variation #1. Have a different well-known character on each card, with that character's "partner" or compliment, on another card. Once they have found their complement, in pantomime or with dialogue, they move off the playing area.

Sample partners: Queen Elizabeth and Prince Philip. Batman and Robin. Superman and Lex Luther. Robin Hood and King John. Winnie the Pooh and Eeyore. Peter Pan and Captain Hook, etc.

Variation #2. Have different animals on the cards. Students move like their animals and make the sounds of their animals, until they find someone else acting like the same animal.

Variation #3: Have different attitudes on the cards. They move around the space, interacting with each other, demonstrating their attitudes until they find someone else with the same attitude.

Sample attitudes: pleased to see everyone, afraid, shy, superior to everyone, suspicious, bored, desperate to find someone, etc.

Variation #4: Have different objectives on cards, with each objective having a matching objective on another card. Students play their objectives until they find someone with the same objective.

Sample objectives: Find out what time it is. Get someone to offer you a piece of candy. Get someone to offer to make a phone call for you. Find someone to sing you a song. Try to take a group picture of everyone together. Get people to offer you a piece of their clothing or jewelry. Get someone to do your homework. You just got some bad news but are trying not to cry. You just got some great news, but want to keep it a secret. Get someone to help you find your contact lens. You have poison ivy, but are trying not to scratch, etc.

Variation #5: Have different objects on the cards. For very young children this could be a picture. Students must "show" their imaginary object by playing with it and inviting others to interact with it in an appropriate manner. All this is done silently, in pantomime, simultaneously as the students move around the playing area. They keep going until someone mimes the same object as they themselves are miming. Then they know that they have found their partner.

Sample objects: ball, hula-hoop, puppy, skateboard, jump rope, lollipop, banana, ghetto blaster, comic book, gerbil, snake, frog, flower, sunglasses, Discman, lip gloss, pair of scissors, etc.

CHANGE THREE THINGS

Method: Students stand back to back with their partners and take turns changing three things about themselves, in terms of clothing, jewelry, hair and so on. They then turn to their partners, who try to list the changes. Switch partners to repeat the exercise.

LUCKY / UNLUCKY

Method: In pairs, students take turns telling a story in which partner "A" always takes a positive outlook on what happens next and partner "B" always gives it a negative spin. For example:

A: Luckily, a boat came along just then.

B: Yes, but it was leaking badly.

A: Luckily, I was chewing gum and used it to patch the leak.

B: Yes, but they weren't strong enough to help me into the boat.

A: Luckily, they had a rope that I could hang onto as they rowed back to shore.

MIRROR IMAGE

This exercise has been popular for a long time. It is a gentle physical warm-up, but more importantly, it teaches students to focus, concentrate and communicate non-verbally.

Method: The partners face each other. One initiates the movement, the other follows it exactly, as if they were looking into a mirror. The objective is to lead slowly enough to allow your partner to keep up, so that the two of you move as one.

Variation #1. In order to practice and perfect this communication, the whole group watches one pair, trying to determine who is leading and who is following.

Variation #2. One person begins to lead, but soon the other takes over. Control is passed back and forth between partners. Non-verbally they take and relinquish control when it feels appropriate to do so.

Variation #3. One partner moves for five seconds, and then stops. The mirror must then imitate the movement exactly. Gradually increase the length of the mimed action before the partner repeats it, working up to a one-minute mime before the partner mirrors it back.

Variation #4. Instead of using abstract movement, an activity (brushing teeth, making a sandwich, etc.) can be mirrored by the partner, or, the first person can mime the activity for one minute, after which his partner imitates the activity as closely as possible, filling the whole minute.

Variation #5. Mirror image can be played by the whole group. One person leaves the room while a leader is selected. He then returns and tries to see who is leading the movement. The group can either stand in a circle, or place themselves randomly about the room. As long as each person can watch any other person, they can follow the movement.

SEEING WITHOUT EYES

These exercises help the students to explore their environment through senses other than sight.

1. Students stand in pairs approximately fifteen feet away from their partners, with nothing between them. One partner closes his eyes; the other partner decides how close she will stand to her partner. On the leader's command, the students with their eyes closed walk toward their partners and try to stop directly in front of them without banging into them.

2. In pairs, one student stands still with her eyes closed. Her partner stands about five feet away from her, slowly and quietly walking in a circle around her. On the command from the leader to stop, she points to where she thinks her partner is before opening her eyes.

NOTE: As no one from another pair can be too close to her, the playing area must be quite large, or students must take turns playing this exercise.

3. Students sit in pairs or small groups and close their eyes. The leader hands one of them a small object, which they pass back and forth between themselves. With their eyes closed they discuss what they think the object is, and then open their eyes to see if they are right.

4. In pairs, one of the partners closes their eyes. The partners with their eyes open find a different partner to sit in front of. The non-sighted partner touches the face of her new partner and tries to guess who it is. She opens her eyes to see if she is right.

Variation #1. Instead of opening their eyes to see if they were right, all sighted partners stand and form a line. Then the rest open their eyes and pick out who they think was their partner. No one speaks up until after the last person has guessed, allowing for the possibility that a student could have been picked by more than one person.

CARRY THE POLE

This exercise focuses not only on mime skills, but also on communication, awareness and concentration.

Method: Each pair mimes carrying a pole, about the size of a broomstick handle, between them as they move around the room. They must be aware of other pairs and not bang into their poles. They can also be instructed to stand the pole on end and circle it, lie it down and pick it up again, or perform any number of other physical actions with their poles. They can also be told that the pole has changed weight. Perhaps it is now made of lead, or spaghetti.

Variation #1. Instead of a pole, there could be an imaginary length of rope between them. They could have a tug of war with it. Teams could be formed for a larger group tug of war.

Variation #2. Instead of a pole, a full bucket of water could be mimed. The pair could pass the bucket to another pair, finally forming a line to pass the buckets to be poured on an imaginary fire at the end of the line.

SIMULTANEOUS SPEECH

This exercise focuses on the students' ability to think spontaneously in order to keep the conversation going. It also requires concentration, as the students try not to become distracted.

Method: In pairs, students are given a topic to debate. On the command to start, they must present their points of view and defend them against their partners' opposing views. The twist is that neither of them stops talking, even for a second, until the leader calls "time." At that point, each student tries to recall what her partner's points were.

Sample arguments: The best pet—dogs or cats
The best place to eat out
The best place to go for vacation
The best (or worst) subject of study

Variation #1. Repeat the exercise, having students switch sides halfway through the argument.

Variation #2. Students work in threes. The student in the middle will be talked at by the other two students at the same time. Each will carry on a different conversation with the middle person, with each wanting something from him. He must be able to keep up with both conversations simultaneously.

Example: Student A wants to borrow his homework, while student B wants him to find out if his brother wants to go out with her. This is quite challenging for the middle person and quite entertaining to watch. It could be done by one trio at a time, rather than having the whole group perform the exercise simultaneously.

TRADING PLACES

This exercise focuses on physicalization, as well as observation.

Method: Students forms pairs and stand facing their partners, who are approximately fifteen feet away. They will number themselves A and B. The leader will call out two words, one for A and another for B. The words are opposites. The pairs will walk slowly towards each other, physicalizing the word they are given. When they pass by each other, they take on their partner's characterization, and discard their own.

Sample word pairs:

Attitudes	happy/sad
	surprised/ bored
	angry/loving
	excited/apathetic
Colours	red/green
	white/black
	blue/yellow
	gray/orange
Ages	five/fifteen
	twenty/forty
	thirty/sixty
	fifty/ninety
Occupations	truck driver/ballet dancer
	lawyer/homeless person
	opera singer/garbage collector
	secretary/farmer

QUICK PHYSICAL PARTNER WARM-UPS

These exercises get the students physically warmed up and ready to work as well as having them interact with and get to know and trust other members of the group. It is important to vary the pairing up each lesson.

1. Back to back: Leader calls out two body parts that must be touching. Starting slowly and symmetrically, the leader progresses at a faster speed and varies the points of contact. Students attempt only one point of contact at a time; they do not add them up cumulatively as they are called out; i.e., "Stand: back to back, side to side, hand to hand, foot to foot. shoulder to shoulder, hand to foot, side to knee, leg to ankle, hand to back, head to shoulder, back to back, foot to elbow," etc.

Variation #1. Have the students find a new partner for each new position.

2. Sit down, stand up: students stand back to back and link arms. They lower themselves to sit on the floor, on their bums, feet out in front, and then attempt to stand up again.

SAFETY NOTE: Do NOT allow students to flip each other over their backs in this standing position. The student on top has no way of bracing himself, should the supporting student crumble. The top student is sure to bang his head on the floor.

3. Touch my back: students try to touch each other's backs while not allowing their partners to touch theirs.

4. Turn me over: one student "grabs the floor" on hands and knees, or lying face down. His partner tries to turn him over.

5. Pinch my penny: Partners sit on the floor facing each other, one hand behind their backs, the other covering a penny on the floor in front of them. Slowly moving their own penny under their hands, they try to snatch their partner's penny without losing their own. This can also be played in groups of four or five.

Variation #1. Partners stand with the penny in a open outstretched left hand. They are only allowed to move from the waist up.

Variation #2. Partners move around the room with the penny in an open hand, trying to grab their partner's penny.

Variation #3. As a further exercise in concentration, they hold a conversation, or go over their lines from a scene, or repeat nursery rhymes simultaneously while performing the penny exercise.

6. Don't drop the toothpick: partners move around the room together, with a toothpick held between them, using only one finger each.

Variation #1. Repeat this exercise with eyes closed.

7. Dance of the tissue: Partners move around the room with two squares of tissue paper held between them with only a thumb and one finger. Players are as imaginative as possible with their movements, trying not to allow the tissue squares to separate.

8. Fluid tableaux—see TABLEAUX EXERCISES

9. Balance the ball: Partners move around the room, balancing a ball between them without using their hands. A body part can be specified (arms only, back to back) or the movement can be left fluid, with each partnership using as much body surface as possible without engaging their hands.

NOTE: Could also be done in a group of three.

---

10. Danger: Students help each other out of some dangerous situation, in pantomimed action or with dialogue added.

Sample situations: A burning building
A narrow mountain ledge
The branches of a tree with a bear
   waiting below
A canoe filling with water
Skiing down a mountain chased
   by an avalanche
In a mine shaft after a cave in
A cargo box on a ship
A pit trap set by hunters

11. Points of contact—see TABLEAUX EXERCISES

12. Off balance; Create an interdependent tableau, in which both partners need each other for balance. Once a tableau is formed, find a way to move across the floor without losing the pose.

Variation #1. Partners find ways to support each other to move creatively across the floor. One person is off balance, needing the other to complete a step, and then roles are immediately reversed as the first student supports the movement of the second.

13. Action/reaction: One partner creates a large movement, which his partner responds to with another movement. They go back and forth responding to each other, creating a sort of dance. These movements could be accompanied by a vocalized sound.

14. Add Four: One partner begins a four-beat (count) movement. The other player repeats it and adds another four-beat movement to it. They take turns until they have an entire movement sequence sixteen to twenty beats in length. Partners can then share them with the class. Various styles of music can be played to inspire the movement.

15. Hypnotic Trance: Partners take turns leading each other by drawing them along with a hand a few feet from their faces. The leader walks backwards in front of her partner, guiding where he should go and whether he should walk low or high, fast or slow, stop or start.

Variation #1. This exercise can be repeated with a small group, and then a larger one. Again, one person draws along the group as they look only at her hand. Repeat, giving new leaders a chance to experience the ultimate in status and control.

16. The Whoosh—See RELAXATION EXERCISES

INDIVIDUAL WARM-UP EXERCISES

Individual warm-ups are practiced near the beginning of each session, in order for each student to physically and mentally prepare for it. This means leaving behind whatever problems or thoughts they brought into the space, in order to focus on the activities to come. These warm-ups can take many forms, but they could be as simple as breathing exercises.

BREATHING EXERCISES

LISTEN TO YOUR BREATH

This simply effective exercise allows students to relax and focus their energy before beginning a lesson.

Method: Have students lie on their backs with their eyes closed. Breathe in to a count of four, hold the breath for a second, and then release to a count of four, again holding the breath for a second before inhaling again.

THE TIGER

There is an ancient oriental martial art which suggests that the three layers of the stratosphere contain creatures from which we can pull or gather energy for our own use. Under the earth are the serpents. On the ground are tigers and in the air are dragons. This breathing exercise utilizes the energy of all three.

Method: Standing with feet shoulder-width apart, spread arms to the side, inhale and circle arms overhead, gathering the energy of the dragon. Exhale while dropping arms and torso forward. Scope the energy of the serpent in a circular motion around the feet and bring it up to the sky with an inhale. Bend knees and bring arms from above the head to the front of the body, pushing them forward, exhaling strongly through the mouth with the energy of a tiger, claws outstretched. Repeat the exercise.

PHYSICAL WARM-UPS

Any stretching or calisthenics exercise can be used to loosen the body and prepare it for further exercises.

SHAKE IT OUT

Method: Students shake each limb in turn, finally dropping from the stomach and shaking out shoulders, allowing their torsos to hang, relaxed.

Variation #1. Young children will enjoy this exercise, with the leader pretending that the limb has a mind of its own. Each limb in turn goes faster and faster, out of control, until it's stopped by grabbing it with the free hand. Finally, the whole body shakes until the child falls to the floor in a heap in an effort to make it stop.

JUMPING JACKS

Method: Start by standing feet together, arms down at the sides. Jump to a position of feet shoulder-width apart and hands clapping overhead. Return to starting position and repeat to a rhythmic count.

ARM CIRCLES

Method: Standing, feet slightly apart, stretch arms horizontally out in front of the body. Slowly circle first one arm up over the top, around, and back to the front. Circle forward, circle backward. Try circling one arm forward and the other backward at the same time.

SHOULDER ROLLS

Method: Standing with feet slightly apart, raise shoulders up towards ears, bring them forward, down, to the back, and up again, slowly rolling them in circles. Go backward as well as forward. Roll one at a time, and then both together to a rhythmic count.

Variation #1. Bring one shoulder up, and then drop it forward. Bring it up and drop it to the back. Try one, then the other, and then both together. Try bringing both shoulders up and dropping one forward and one backward at the same time. Repeat, reversing which shoulder drops forward and which one drops to the back. Repeat with arms horizontally out to the sides. When a shoulder drops forward, the hand faces backwards. When a shoulder drops backwards, the palm of the hand faces the ceiling.

REACH AND DROP

Method: Standing with feet shoulder-width apart, reach the right arm straight up to the ceiling. Reach the left arm even higher, repeat once with each arm. Then drop everything down to the floor, both sides together, one body part at a time:

> Hands from the wrists
> Forearms from the elbows
> Upper arms from the shoulder
> Head
> Shoulders
> Upper back
> Lower back from the waist

Hang, relaxing shoulders, arms, neck and head, for a count of four. Then slowly rise, beginning with the lower back, straightening up one vertebra at a time, with the head the last to come up. Reach for the ceiling with the right hand to begin the exercise again. The exercise is done to a count of eight:

> 1-2-3-4 to stretch arms up, one at a time
> 5-6-7-8 drop hands, forearms, upper arms, head
> 1-2-3-4 drop from the shoulders, upper back,
>   lower back, waist
> 5-6-7-8 hang, loosely shaking out the shoulders
> 1-2-3-4-5-6-7-8 slowly roll up to begin again

TWISTS

Method: Standing with feet shoulder-width apart, arms horizontally out to the side, twist torso to each side, looking behind. Bend knees slightly to protect them. Let arms relax, slapping the sides of the body at the end of the swing.

Variation #1. Bend forward at the waist, back straight, touching one hand to the opposite toes; with the other hand high above head, repeat to other side.

ROCK AND ROLL

Method: Sit back on haunches, bum off the floor, arms wrapped around knees. Roll back to lie on floor, feet still curled in original position, close to the body. Trying not to put hands on the floor, roll back up onto feet.

PHYSICAL COORDINATION EXERCISES

These exercises are fun to try and not too difficult to master. They will warm up the students physically and improve their general coordination.

1. **Method:** Sequence is done to a count of eight:

   1. Feet astride, arms out to the side. (half a jumping jack).
   2. Feet together, hands clap overhead.
   3. Feet astride, arms to the side (position #1).
   4. Feet together, arms down.
   5. Feet astride, hands clap overhead (a full jumping jack).
   6. Feet together, arms down (position #4).
   7. Raise one knee, clap beneath it.
   8. Feet together, arms down (position #4).

   Repeat the sequence, building up speed.

2. **Method:** Sequence is done with arms only.

   The right arm works to a count of four, describing (punching out) four positions in the air, out to the side:

   1. Arm up.
   2. Arm three quarters of the way up.
   3. Arm three quarters of the way down.
   4. Arm down.

   The left arm works to a count of two:

   1. Arm up.
   2. Arm down.

   Now work both arms at once, each following its own sequence. When that becomes easy, switch the sequence, counting four on the left and two on the right.

Variation #1. Have one arm describe three positions in the air, while the other describes two. Now try for three and four.

FIVE TABLEAUX

(see TABLEAUX section for explanation of tableaux). This exercise teaches students to allow their bodies to retain the memory of the positions they have held. It is also a great energizing physical warm-up.

Method: Students create a single tableau, then another and another until they have five of them. Encourage students to go through each of them one at a time to remember them in order. Then, call out the numbers in sequence for them to perform them simultaneously, before calling them out in random order as they remember which tableau went with which number.

LEAP UP

While this looks like a physical exercise, it actually requires more mental focusing than physical prowess.

Method: The students kneel and sit back on their heels (best done in socking feet, not shoes). They focus all of their energy in the solar plexus, and then, when ready, explode from sitting back on their knees to their feet, in a crouching position. It is not as difficult as it sounds and almost everyone can do it on the first try.

PHYSICAL WARM-UPS USING THE IMAGINATION

Instead of counting out the rhythm of an exercise, a physical warm-up can have the students imagine themselves in a situation requiring a physical response. The following exercises are fashioned with this in mind. They are performed as pantomimes, stories without words.

ELASTIC BAND

Method: Students pretend to have an enormous elastic band, big enough to be stretched between their feet and upraised arms.

The leader narrates the experience of stretching the band into many different configurations requiring physical movements. All students work independently, simultaneously.

Sample narration: Pick your elastic band up off of the floor. Give it a shake. Hold it out in front of you and put it around one foot. Stretch that foot down to the floor. Reach your arm up over your head, stretching the band as far as it will go. Careful, don't let it snap. Oh, it snapped, You're down on the floor in a heap. Ouch, that's got to hurt. Pick it up again, careful now. Stay down on the floor. Curl into a ball. Stretch the band around your hands and feet. Now stretch your hands and feet out to the side as far as you can....and so on.

ATMOSPHERE WALKS

These walks through different atmospheres act as a physical warm-up and develop the students' sense of their own bodies and how to control their movements. It also develops their imaginations.

Method: The leader narrates the group through experiences with different kinds of atmospheres. All students work independently, simultaneously.

Sample atmospheres:

Walk through a field of corn, pushing plants aside with every step.
Walk on the moon, with less gravity than the earth.
Walk through walls of sticky taffy.
Walk through cotton candy, marshmallows or a vat of jellybeans.
Swim through a thick milkshake or soup.
Swim through a crystal clear lake, magically breathing underwater.
Walk on fluffy clouds, sinking and floating at the same time.

ESCAPE

Method: The leader narrates the group through experiences of trying to escape from something. Students work independently, simultaneously.

Sample entrapments:

> A dolphin trapped in a fishing net.
> A Butterfly caught in a net.
> A bear caught in a trap.
> A child stuck in a well.
> A mouse cornered by a cat.
> A customer accidentally trapped in a bathroom
>   by a broken lock.
> A genie trapped in a magic lamp.

CAPTURE

Method: The leader narrates the group through experiences of trying to catch an imaginary something or someone. Students work independently, simultaneously.

Sample scenarios:

> A fisherman struggling to land a fish.
> A cowpoke trying to rope a calf.
> An animal trainer trying to coax a lion back
>   into its cage.
> A babysitter trying to get a child into bed.
> An elegant businessperson flagging down a cab
>   at rush hour.

INDIVIDUAL PANTOMIME

One or two of the following exercises can be done independently, simultaneously by members of the group as a warm-up to more involved pantomime exercises.

Become:

> A candle that is lit and slowly burns down.
> A bud that opens into a flower.
> A puppet on strings.

A cat waking up from a nap.
A jack-in-the-box that pops open.
A child jumping over a lawn sprinkler.
A spinning top.
A yo-yo.
A bouncing ball.
A puppy doing tricks for treats.
A young chick breaking out of its shell.
A pen gliding across the page, writing your name.
A fish caught in a net.

Pretend to:

Blow up a huge balloon that carries you into the sky.
Chase a butterfly and catch it in your hands.
  Then let it go.
Be a safe-cracker, listening for the combination.
Open a closet that is too full of things.
Make a milkshake in a blender.
Make a basket from the foul line.
Dance the victory dance after a touchdown.
Put on the greatest outfit and model it on a runway.
Fly a kite without enough wind.
Make your way through a field filled with land mines.

CLASSIC CHARADES

Method: Students form two teams. Teams send up one member per round to look at the word on a card held by the leader, before acting out the word (or phrase) for his group. The team that guesses the correct word or phrase first gets a point. Have teams sit as far apart as space allows.

Sample phrases:

Broken violin string	Snow-capped mountain
Old torn sneaker	New spinning top
Fountain of youth	Overdue library book
Burned-out lightbulb	Christmas tree lights

Variation #1. Instead of phrases, movie, book or TV show titles could be used.

WHERE AM I?

Method: Students are asked to lie down and pretend to sleep. On the command from the leader, they wake up and find themselves in an unfamiliar environment. They don't recall how they got there. They explore their new surroundings and may speak aloud to (imaginary) people that they find there.

Sample environments:

> A seaside report
> A downtown back alley
> A sheik's tent out in the desert
> A haunted house
> A dark forest
> The hull of a ship

ANIMAL

Method: Each student becomes an animal of her choice and narrates the birth, babyhood, adulthood, old age and death of the animal. Everyone works independently, but simultaneously, speaking aloud to him or herself while pantomiming the life of the animal. Some narration by the leader may be necessary to assist students in reaching the next stage in the life of the animal.

TRUST-BUILDING EXERCISES

Trust exercises are very important when the group is newly formed. Trust needs to be established between members in order for them to feel that they are in a safe enough environment to take chances with their imaginations.

CIRCLE SIT

This exercise requires that everyone work together.

Method: All students form a tight circle, turn to their right and take another step in towards the centre of the circle. Students should be almost touching. On the count of three, all students sit on the knees of the person behind them. On the count of three, they stand up again. With practice, they can also take three steps forward (or backwards) while they sit. The first time, students may wish to perform this while holding the shoulders of the student in front of them.

BLIND WALK

The object of this exercise is to learn to trust the partner who is guiding, and to learn to become trustworthy. For beginners, use a large open space. For a more advanced group, use a space in which an obstacle course of boxes, chairs or other objects has been created.

Explanation to Group: You and your partner will take turns leading each other through this space. Your objective is to keep your partner safe at all times. Have your partner take your arm, close their eyes and allow you to lead them through the room. Keep talking to them, telling them when to turn, step up or get around any obstacle.

Variations #1. Instead of having your "blind" partner take your arm, you take hold of her elbow, guiding her at your side without talking at all.

Variation #2. Don't touch your partner at all. Guide him only with your voice, telling him where and when to step.

Variation #3. Instead of speaking to your partner, decide on a repetitive sound that he will follow through the space.

ENCHANTED FOREST

This in another way of creating the space for the Blind Walk. Instead of making an obstacle course of objects, half of the group becomes trees in an enchanted forest. The trees watch for the partners and make interesting tableaux for them to navigate as they pass through the forest.

TRUCKS

Fun at any age, this game is a variation of the traditional "Blind Walk" trust exercise.

Method: In pairs, one partner is the driver and the other is the truck. The truck closes her eyes. Drivers move their trucks through the space, avoiding collisions with other trucks. Drivers do not speak. They give their trucks signals, telling them where to go. A continuous tap on the top of the head means go forward. A tap on the left shoulder is a left turn; right shoulder, right turn. Continuous tapping on the back is reverse. If the tapping stops, the truck stops. The objective is for the drivers to keep their trucks safe, enabling the trucks to trust their drivers. After a few minutes, the roles are reversed and play begins again.

RUN THE GAUNTLET

Method: Students form one long line and raise one arm above their heads. The person at the end of the line runs past all the rest, as quickly and as close to them as she dares. Each person in line drops his or her arm down just before she reaches it. Sounds simple but is actually quite scary.

Variation #1. If the group is big enough, over thirty members, two lines could be formed, with the person running down the centre. This is more exciting, but won't work if the group is so small that the line becomes too short.

PENCILS

This exercise should only be played with an older group of students, once they are ready for it.

Method: Students form groups of six or seven. Students take turns lying on the floor in the middle of their group, stiff as pencils, crossing their arms over their chests. Group members gather around the supine person. Slowly the group lifts the student, every group member responsible for one part of her body, helping her feel confident in their support. She is lifted above the shoulders of the rest of her group and carried around the room. After a few minutes, they gently waft her back and forth while slowly lowering her to the floor.

PING-PONG BALL

This exercise is also fairly advanced and should not be attempted with students that are not mature enough to handle it.

Method: In groups of six or seven, students take turns standing in the centre of their circle, feet firmly together and planted on the floor, arms crossed over chest. The group forms a tight circle, with each member standing in a lunge position, one foot into the centre of the circle for stability. Staying very straight, the centre student falls towards the outside of the group, caught by the person lunging there, who gently passes him to the next person or across the circle. Everyone must stay focused and ready to help the person beside him or her. The centre person will try to keep his eyes closed.

FREE FALL

This exercise is only for advanced students who have already built up a basic level of trust with each other.

Method: A student stands on a chair or table and falls forward or back, caught by four other players. The student must remember to keep his arms outstretched sideways during the fall, as he will be caught by a player on each side facing the table, ready to place one hand at the faller's armpit and another at his wrist. The remaining two catchers are at the faller's legs. The student should call out before falling, so the catchers can be ready.

CONCENTRATION EXERCISES

Concentration is a very important skill in acting, whether in improvised situations or when working with scripts. A student needs to maintain concentration, or focus, in the scene in order to stay in character and to learn to listen to what the other characters are saying.

LISTEN TO THE ROOM

This is concentration in its simplest form.

Method: Students lie on their backs with their eyes closed. They are asked to listen to whatever sounds they can hear outside of the classroom. Once they have voiced what they heard, they are asked to close their eyes again and focus on what they can hear inside their classroom. The next objective is to focus on what they can hear inside their own bodies. They will report hearing their breathing, perhaps a cough or a swallow. They may hear (feel) their heartbeats. Follow this exercise with some breathing or relaxation exercises.

THE CLAP

This exercise focuses on cooperation and concentration.

Method: The group stands in a circle. Each person claps once, directly followed by the person beside him, creating a wave effect.

Variation #1. As a concentration exercise, a pattern can be established, with two players clapping once each and every third person clapping twice, keeping this pattern going around the circle. (Or have a pattern of three or four single claps, followed by a double.)

Variation #2. As a concentration exercise, the pattern can build with each person. The first person claps once, the second person claps twice, the third claps once, the fourth twice and so on.

Variation #3. Each person claps with the person on each side of him. This means that there will always be three people clapping at one time, as the sound moves around the circle.

KEEP THE BEAT

The purpose of this game is to keep the beat, remember your number and use it appropriately. The focus is on concentration and coordination.

Method: The group sits on the floor in a circle. The leader is also part of the circle, but on a chair. The person on the chair is the king or queen of the game. (Once the game is well known, a student can begin as monarch.) The students are all numbered, beginning with the person on the monarch's right. It is everyone's aim to become king or queen. This is done by moving up a number whenever someone above you breaks the rhythm. The rhythm is made by everyone in unison: slapping their thighs once, clapping once and snapping their fingers twice (slap, clap, snap, snap). On the first snap, a person says his or her own number. On the second snap, they say someone else's number (or queen). If the person called does not respond on the very next snap, he must move down to the number one spot. Everyone below him now moves up a number. If the king or queen misses the beat, he or she becomes number one and the highest number becomes the monarch.

Variation #1. Instead of numbers, the exercise can be used early in the sessions as a name game. A student calls out his name on the first snap and another name on the second. It could be played with or without the king and queen, moving back to the first spot when they miss.

Variation #2. Instead of numbers, students give themselves a fruit name. This variation is easier, because they would keep these names throughout the game, instead of changing every time a person above them missed the beat. They would still move around the circle, trying to get to the seat of the king or queen, going back to the first spot if they miss the beat.

Variation #3. Instead of using numbers, each student chooses an animal. They must have a sound and a hand posture to represent that animal. Best played in small groups, it is perhaps the most difficult of the variations, requiring players to demonstrate their sound and posture on the first snap and someone else's on the second; sample posture: saying, "Ruff," and putting both "paws" up in a begging position would represent a dog.

CIRCLE STORY

The focus is on concentration and spontaneity.

Method: The group sits on the floor in a circle. A story is told one word at a time, with each student adding his or her own word to the one before theirs. There should be no pauses between words. While the story can be silly, the syntax should be correct.

Variation #1. The game can be played with elimination rounds. If a word is given that doesn't fit the syntax of the sentence, or the pause before a word is given is too long, that person is out of the circle and the rest continue to play until only one person remains.

Variation #2. Instead of everyone adding just one word, each student must repeat all the words that came before, adding their own word on at the end.

Variation #3. The story can be told in one sentence, instead of a word at a time. However, instead of completing a sentence, each person stops in the middle of a sentence and allows the next person to finish that sentence and begin a new one.

Variation #4. Each person continues the story with three or four sentences, again allowing the next person to finish the thought. This can be played as GIVE or TAKE. In GIVE, a person stops mid-thought and gives the story to the next person. In TAKE, the next person takes away the story from the last teller when he wants to interject his own idea.

Variation #5. The leader gives the group a sentence that has as many words as there are students in the circle. Once it has been repeated as a group several times, one word is assigned to each person in the circle. They practice saying the sentence until it flows smoothly, as if only one person were speaking.

Variation #6. In small groups, a story is told around the circle. Once a story is finished, a narrator retells it for the whole group, with the other small group members miming the action.

WHAT'S MY FRUIT?

Method: Students sit on the floor in a circle. Each student chooses the name of a fruit, which they keep throughout the exercise. One student stands in the centre of the circle holding a rolled-up newspaper or soft sponge baseball bat. One seated student begins by naming his own fruit and someone else's. That student must respond with his own fruit and someone else's before the player in the middle can get to him and bop him on the head with the newspaper. If he gets bopped before finishing his response, he goes into the centre. If he gets his response out, the play continues and the centre person goes after the next player named.

It sounds violent, but is really a lot of fun.

Variation #1. Instead of using fruit names, animals can be named, with a tableau accompaniment. For example, placing the hands on the head for ears could represent a rabbit. To make this exercise even more difficult, it could be done non-verbally, using only the tableau symbols.

FRUIT BASKET UPSET—see LOW ORGANIZED GAMES

SAY MY NAME—see NAME GAMES

PASS THE OBJECT

Method: Students stand in a circle. One student is chosen to stand in the centre with his eyes closed. A small object is passed from hand to hand around the circle until the centre student calls, "stop." He gives the player caught with the object a letter of the alphabet. The object is again passed around the circle while the student caught tries to name six nouns that begin with that letter. If she succeeds, play continues. If she does not, she goes into the centre of the circle for the next round.

Variation #1. The student with the object tries to name as many objects as possible before the object returns to her. She then automatically goes to the centre. Each student tries to name more objects than the current record number.

Variation #2. The student caught with the object gives the student in the centre a letter. He must give at least six nouns beginning with that letter before the object goes around again. If he is successful, he takes the place of that student on the outside. If not, he stays in the centre for another round.

SPEECH IN A MINUTE

Method: Each student takes a turn to pick from a deck of cards, each cards contains one word. They then have exactly one minute to give the group a speech based on that word. They must fill the whole minute. They pick the card only when it is their turn to speak.

Sample words: Fire, paint, window, colour, run, sleep, doors, pain, fly, date, and study.

FAMOUS NAMES

Method: Students sit in a circle. One person begins by naming any famous person. The next person names another famous person, whose first name begins with the same letter as the beginning of the last person's last name; e.g., Winston Churchill, Charlie Chaplain, Charles Bronsen, Bobby Fisher, etc.

Variation #1. Instead of famous people, students name bodies of water. Each name must begin with the last letter of the name before it. Other categories to use: towns and cities, kinds of candy and junk food, makes and models of cars.

NAME THE OBJECT   This is A what?

Method: Students sit in a circle. Each student holds a small personal object; a pen, cup, book, key, etc. One student begins by holding her object out for the person on her right, saying, "This is a pen." The next person responds with, "A what?" The first person repeats, "A pen." Second person, "A what?" First person, "A pen." Second person, "Oh, a pen." The second person takes the pen and repeats the conversation with the next person to his right. The next object is brought into play immediately by the student on the first person's left. Gradually, more objects are brought into play, with the first objects going around a second and third time. Finally everyone is trying to hold two conversations with two different people, about two different objects, at the same time. Or, all objects can be introduced at the same time.

Variation #1. Instead of using many objects, only two are used; one goes to the right and one to the left. Two students sitting side by side in the circle begin them. The exercise is complicated by needing the question, "A what?" to go all the way back to the first student each time a new person is asked. The response must also go back along the line, repeated by each person in turn.

MAKE A LIST

This exercise focuses on concentration and memory.

Method: Sitting in a circle, students take turns saying what they will bring on a camping trip. Each student must remember to say everything that has come before him or her before adding their own item; e.g., first student: "I went on a camping trip and took a tent." Second student, "I went on a camping trip and took a tent and my sleeping bag," etc.

Variation #1. Instead of a camping trip, any other experience can be used that necessitates a different equipment list; e.g.,

> "I work in an office and use—my computer, a pen, some files, a phone, paper," etc.

> "I built a building and used—wood, cement, a hammer, a saw, nails," etc.

> "I went to the mall and saw—my friends, clothes, the food court, an escalator, the information desk," etc.

> "I visited the zoo and I saw—a zebra, some monkeys, a kangaroo, a zookeeper, a baby in stroller, a guy selling cotton candy," etc.

Variation #2. Instead of this being a verbal exercise, each student creates a sound and single movement. The next person must repeat all the other sounds and movements in the order given before adding his own.

WORD ASSOCIATION

Method: In pairs, one player repeats the word given by the leader. Her partner responds with the first word that comes to mind. After a minute, the leader calls to stop the exercise and invites the pairs to share their last word with the whole group to illustrate how many directions one word can take. A new word is given to begin the exercise again. This can also be played with small groups. Every player takes a turn to respond, around the circle.

Variation #1. Instead of free association, lists are made of words that fit a certain category, given by the leader; e.g., boys', or girls' names, spices, rivers and lakes, breeds of dogs, names of rock bands, etc. The partners take turns adding to the list. Once they have run out of words, they sit down, indicating that they are finished.

NAME THAT TUNE

Method: Students sit in groups of five or six. Each student decides on a popular tune to hum or whistle. Everyone begins together, with his or her own tune. After a minute they all stop and try to identify the other tunes in their group.

Variation #1. Instead of sitting in a group, all students walk around freely in the playing area. At the end of the exercise, they identify as many tunes as possible, heard while they circulated and kept up with their own tune.

JUST CAN'T SMILE

There are many exercises in which the only objective to keep a straight face. The theory is that being able to control whether or not you break out with a smile will later help with concentration playing a role in a scene. Perhaps, but more likely a true focus on the role will do that easily enough. These exercises are simply fun to play.

PARTNER STARING MATCHES

Method: Partners sit opposite each other and try, in turn, to make each other smile. Anything goes except physical contact. This can be done in a fairly short time, as a round robin competition. As players are eliminated they become audience—at very close range. It makes the rounds go even faster.

NAP TIME

Method: All players lie on their backs for "nap time" except one, who moves through the area and tries to make those lying down smile or laugh. They must make eye contact. If they smile, they stand and help make others laugh, until no one is left lying down.

CUTE BABY

Method: All students sit in a circle except one, who is in the middle. This student approaches anyone in the circle with the words, "You're the cutest baby in the whole wide world, won't you give me a smile?" The student approached must make eye contact the entire time and respond with, "I know that I'm the cutest baby in the whole wide world, but I just can't smile." If the student smiles, she goes into the centre. If, after approaching three students, she cannot get anyone to smile, the fourth one automatically goes in to replace her.

HAGOO

The Flingit First Nations of Alaska invented this game. The word "Hagoo" means, "Come here". It's an opportunity for students to try out their best comedy material in order to make each other laugh. The objective of the individual player is to walk the gauntlet without laughing or smiling.

Method: Students line up in two rows, facing each other. One player from each team stands at the end of the space between the lines and bows deeply to the player at the other end. Both repeat the word "Hagoo" before walking towards each other. Players on each side try to make the other team's player laugh as they pass by. No physical contact is allowed. If they succeed, that player joins their team. If they reach the end of the line without laughing, they go back to their own teams. Play continues until every player has had a turn, or, if time permits, until one team has all the players.

INTERROGATION

Method: Students sit in a circle with one player in the centre who will ask a question of any student on the outside. When the question is asked, the two students must maintain eye contact, but it is the student to the left of the one questioned who actually answers the question. The student speaking will try to make the other two laugh. Whoever laughs goes to the centre. If no one does, the interrogator goes to another person. Keep the exercise moving as quickly as possible.

THE EMPIRE

This concentration game is also a great introduction to the concept of status.

Method: One player is selected to begin the game as the Emperor/Empress. He or she is the only one in a chair, with the rest of the subjects sitting in the circle on the floor. The ruler has absolute power over the subjects. They may not speak or even shift position with asking permission. They do this by raising their hands, asking to stand, and then asking to speak. If granted the right to speak, they again ask before sitting down. As this is a concentration game, they may not laugh or even smile. If someone does smile, another subject may tell the ruler, who then decides on a suitable punishment, which might be to sing a song, or do push-ups. All subjects are numbered and can only be called by their right title, which is Subject One, Subject Two and so on. It is also their job to please the ruler. They can do so by offering compliments and telling him or her what others are doing that might displease the ruler. The ruler can change their numbers at will, rewarding them with a higher ranking, or punishing them by moving them down. The only way to get rid of the ruler is to catch him or her smiling or calling a subject by the incorrect number. In this case a subject appeals to the judge, the leader, who is outside the game. The leader can remove the ruler and appoint the highest-numbered subject as the new Emperor/Empress.

STUPID TRICKS

Stupid tricks are just that and it is best to name them before the students do. They are very simple, but only after you know what the trick is. They are, perhaps, the ultimate observation games. Encourage your students to try out their theories once they think they have the trick, but ask them to please resist the temptation to share the answer with their neighbours. Instead, they can help the rest of the group to catch on by demonstrating the correct answer when their turn comes.

ROAD TRIP

The purpose of this game is to figure out why something can or cannot be taken along on this road trip.

Method: The group sits in a circle. The leader begins by saying, "We are going on a road trip and I am taking along ___" and takes something that begins with the first letter of her name. If this class is in a school where the class calls the teacher by her surname, use that; e.g., Ms Smith takes a sandwich. If this game is played near the beginning of a new session, it can be used as a name game. That way the students are given a clue to the game's answer and they are being helped to remember each other's names. The bonus is that the leader knows whether or not the students give a correct answer, whether or not she already knows everyone's name. Ask them to say their first names and what they are bringing along.

Variation #1. The object must begin with the last letter of the last object, (whether it was correct or not); e.g., sandwich, hammer, rock, kitten, necktie, and so on.

Variation #2. The object must be a word with three letters (or four, or five).

Variation #3. The object must be a word with a double letter; e.g., kitten, butter.

Variation #4. The object must begin with the same letter as the first name of the person on your left (or right).

TAKE A PICTURE

The purpose of this game is to guess who the leader took a picture of. It is quite easy and suitable for younger children.

Method: The group sits around the room on the floor, preferably not in a rigid circle. One person leaves the room, after which the leader pretends to take a picture of one of the students. The person returns and has three guesses as to who had their picture taken. The leader will sit exactly like the person whose picture was taken. Allow other students to leave the room as they decide they know how to correctly guess.

DRAW A FACE

The purpose of this game is to find the "correct" way to draw an imaginary face on the floor in front of you, with the stick that is passed around.

Method: The group sits in a circle. The leader tells the class that she is going to draw a face. She then clears her throat and draws an imaginary face, describing the features as she draws. Then the stick is passed to the next person and he is asked to draw a face. The simple trick is to clear your throat before you draw your choice of face.

Variation #1. Instead of drawing a face, you could use a long pole, banging it on the floor as you repeat any nonsense rhyme, such as: "Peanut butter, peanut butter, I love peanut butter. Peanut butter, peanut butter, I eat it every day." Again, it doesn't matter how you hold the pole or how you say the rhyme, but only that you clear your throat before you start.

WHO'S GOT THE BALL?

The purpose of this game is to figure out who is holding the imaginary ball after the leader has tossed it.

Method: The leader mimes tossing the ball to one, two or any other number of students, who are sitting around her in a circle on the floor. The leader says, "Toss," each time she mimes throwing the ball to a different student. When she has finished tossing it to as many students as she likes (or none at all—she could simply toss it into the air above her head, just to throw them off track), she puts her hands in her lap and asks, "Who's got the ball?" Students make their guesses. What they don't know is that the person with the ball is the first to speak after the leader has asked the question. At first, she will wait for a few more people to speak after the first one before announcing who, in fact, has the ball. After a while, when she wants to start giving hints as to what the trick is and wants it to be more obvious, she could say to the first speaker, who names someone else, "No, Tom doesn't have the ball, you do."

CROSSED/UNCROSSED

The purpose of this game is to receive a pair of scissors from the person beside you and pass them to the next person, determining correctly whether you received them crossed or uncrossed, and how you passed them on.

Method: The group sits in a circle, preferably on chairs. The leader takes a pair of scissors, holds them up and tells the class if she received them crossed or uncrossed. She then passes them to the next person, saying she is passing them crossed (or uncrossed). The simple trick is that the scissors are irrelevant; it is only the position of your feet (legs, knees) that are either crossed or uncrossed when you receive or pass them. As this game is quite difficult, people who know the trick may finally have to be become quite obvious about crossing or uncrossing their knees between receiving and passing them along.

BLACK MAGIC

This game pretends to work because of telepathic powers. The leader can make a great show of having these powers as she leads the game. She chooses one student to take aside to "discover" that they do indeed both share the same telepathic power and are able to read each other's minds. Actually, the leader is teaching her the trick: simply, that the leader will point to something black before pointing to the object that the class has chosen.

Method: Send the person who shares the "power" out of the room while the class decides on an object in the room. Call the student in, make a show of connecting your minds, then begin pointing to different objects, asking the person if this is the object chosen by the class. Directly after pointing to something black, point to the object chosen. The person should correctly identify it. As students believe that they have figured out the trick, allow them to leave the room while the object is chosen in order to test their theory. Continue until most of the students have caught on to the trick.

NOTE: Students will be busy looking for a pattern; e.g., how many objects are pointed to first; how the pointer stick is held when pointing to the right object; what is said each time ("is it this? is it that?"). The leader may have to finally get very obvious; e.g., "Is it that BLUE sweater? Is it this RED cap? Is it this BLACK bag? Is it this?" This trick is so good it can sometimes be played over a period of days before anyone catches on.

PICK A CARD

Like Black Magic, this game pretends to use telepathic powers. Once one student has been taught the trick, the leader is ready to use the powers.

Method: The group sits on the floor in a circle. In front of the leader are nine pieces of plain paper (if this were a very small group, it could be played on a tabletop with playing cards). The "cards" are in three lines of three. The "partner" leaves the room, or closes her eyes, while someone in the group picks a card by pointing to it. The partner returns and the leader points (with a stick) to any one of the cards, asking if this is the one picked. The trick is to treat that first card pointed to as a map or chart for the whole layout. Mentally divide that first card into nine sections, and point to the quadrant that represents the placement of the card picked; e.g., if the middle card was picked, point to the middle of the first card touched. If the leader touches the middle left side of the first card, the correct card is in the middle row, on the left side. After correctly pointing to the first card, it doesn't matter how many others are pointed to, or where, before pointing to the correct one.

NOTE: The leader can even point to the correct card first, by pointing to the correct spot on that card. The partner can also be asked to verbally identify the correct card, after the leader has correctly pointed it out on the first card. This trick can baffle the best of them for a long time.

Point to the correct spot on the first card.

RELAXATION EXERCISES

These exercises can be incorporated into any lesson in which students need to take a few moments to relax and calm down. They can also be combined to create an entire relaxation class.

BREATHING EXERCISES—See INDIVIDUAL WARM-UPS

ROLL OVER

In this exercise, students learn to completely release all muscle tension and allow their bodies to completely relax.

Method: Students lie on the floor, on their backs. The objective is to roll from their backs to their stomachs and back again, without resistance. The roll is done very slowly, by first draping one arm across the front of the body and slowly pulling the rest of the body with it. Once on their stomachs, students begin the roll to their backs by first raising one shoulder.

THE WHOOSH

This partner breathing/massage exercise is also great as a warm-up at the beginning of a lesson; it is energizing and invigorating, as well as relaxing.

Method: In pairs, One student inhales deeply and exhales, dropping forwards from the waist. As she slowly rolls up, one vertebra at a time, she releases her breath to the sound of "Ahhhhhhhhhh." As she rises, her partner, who is standing beside/behind her, rapidly taps her firmly on the back with a cupped hand, being careful not to tap right on her spine. Once she is standing upright, her partner stops tapping, finishing the exercise with one long stoke of both hands along her back, one each side of her spine, from her shoulders to her waist. This "whoosh" at the end feels both relaxing and energizing.

MUSCLE RELAXATION

The theory involved in this exercise is that people can isolate the tension that they carry in specific parts of their bodies, and then release it and allow that muscle to relax. In this way, they can achieve total relaxation.

Method: Students lie comfortably on their backs as the leader narrates them through the exercise, asking them to concentrate on one muscle group at a time. Once the muscle has been identified, it is tensed, with the muscle held tightly for a count of five, then released completely.

Sample narration: Let's start with your feet. Concentrate on your toes. Curl them up as tightly as you can, but don't curl your whole foot, just your toes. Hold that curl...a little longer...and release it. Now flex your foot, but try to leave your toes relaxed. Hold it...a little longer...and release. Circle your feet once to the left. Now once to the right. Make sure that they are completely relaxed. Now try to tense your calf muscles. They are on the back of your lower legs. Try keeping them tensed without tensing your upper legs or your feet. And relax. Now try to isolate your knees. I know that it is almost impossible. Just think about your knees and ignore the rest of your legs. Think about tensing your knees. Now relax them. You have two major muscle groups in your upper legs. On the front of your thigh are your quadriceps. Tense them, but try not to involve your hamstrings, which are on the back of your thighs. Hold the tension in your quads. Now release them and relax. Now go to the back of your thighs and tense your hamstrings. It's hard to isolate them from the quads. Just put your focus on them. Now relax them. Now we'll isolate the biggest muscle group in your whole body, your gluteus maximus; your butt. Put tension in your butt muscles. Hold it...and relax. On your stomach you have abdominal muscles. Try pushing your stomach against the floor to put tension in them. Hold it...and release. On the sides of your chest cavity you will find your latissimus dorsi, your lats. Try to isolate them from the front of your chest and tense them up. Hold it...and relax. Now hold your breath for a moment and push just your upper chest against the floor. Wait, and breathe, relax. Squeeze your hands into a fist. Squeeze them...hold...and relax. Now try to just tense your forearms, but keep your upper arms relaxed. That's hard to do. It is really more of a mental exercise than a physical possibility. Just concentrate on your forearms, from your wrists to your elbows. Now relax them. Your upper arm has a muscle group on the front and another on the back. On the front are your biceps. Try to tense only that group, while leaving your triceps, on the back, relaxed. Hold the biceps...and relax. Now tense the triceps on the back of your upper arms. Tense them...and relax. Pull your shoulders up to your ears. Hold them there. Now let them fall back down. Pull them up again. See how the tension feels. Lots of people carry their shoulders up or forward all the time. If you slouch a lot, carrying all that tension in your neck and shoulders, you may get a lot of headaches. Let your shoulders fall. Roll them a little and make sure that they are very relaxed. Now tense your neck, but try to leave your shoulders and head relaxed. Hold the tension...now relax your neck. Press your head against the floor. Tense it...now release your head and relax. Now let's work on the little muscle groups on your face. Squeeze your eyes shut tightly. Sometimes, when we have trouble getting to sleep, we may squeeze our eyes shut tightly, instead of relaxing and letting them close. Concentrating on relaxing them can sometimes help us fall asleep. Now relax your eyes. Wrinkle your nose and hold it...now relax your nose. Smile as big as you can. Hold that smile...now relax your mouth. Take a deep breath and relax. Now, for a moment, tense your whole body. Squeeze every muscle. Go completely rigid. Hold that tension for another moment...and relax. Release everything. Take a deep breath and release it slowly. Allow every part of your body to completely relax.

SPHERE OF LIGHT

While the previous exercise is completely physical, this exercise has the same effect in terms of totally relaxing the body, but it is completely mental in nature.

Method: Have students lie comfortably on their backs. Narrate them through the experience of having a sphere of light gently massage every part of the bodies from the inside.

Sample narration: Close your eyes. Now imagine that there is a ball, or sphere of white light hovering right above your forehead. See it in your mind's eye. It's round and bright, about the size of a grapefruit. Now imagine that it has entered your head through your forehead. Feel it spinning very fast in a clockwise direction.

Let it rest behind your eyes, spinning and bright. Feel the warmth of the light as it gently massages your eyes. Let it spin down to your cheeks. Feel the warmth as it massages your cheeks. Let it rest at the back of your neck...and so on. Bring the sphere to every part of their bodies in turn. When it goes down one leg, it can pop out of their toes and hop across to the toes of their other foot and go up that leg. Finally bring it back up to their foreheads and either allow it to pop out of their foreheads and dissipate into the air, or allow it to leave their bodies in a deep breath of air from their mouths.

IMAGINARY TRIPS

If a change is as good as rest, an imaginary trip to another place has to be calming and refreshing. It is a good way to help students focus their energies before another exercise, or to relax after other activities and increase their sensory awareness. Having a safe calm environment in which to go for a moment can even release tension and calm nerves in a stressful situation, such as just before a performance, or writing an exam or preparing to enter a room for an interview.

Method: Students lie comfortably on a towel or mat. The lights are dimmed and soft music may be played. The leader takes the students on an imaginary journey. The destination isn't important, as long as it's calm and relaxing, with plenty of soothing imagery. It is important to evoke all of the student's senses in this new location in order to help them really feel that they are in this environment. The leader narrates them through the trip. Various means of travel can also be narrated, in order for students to get from one environment to another. For example, the students can imagine that they are so light that they rise up off the floor and are able to float through the sky. Or they could imagine that they are inside a giant bubble that allows them to float around, even under water.

Sample narrations:

1. Imagine that you are lying on a warm sandy beach. The sun is shinning and you feel so warm. You have been lying there so long that your body has formed an indentation in the

sand. You feel totally supported by the sand. You are so relaxed, so comfortable. You can hear the seagulls calling to each other as they fly out over the ocean. You hear the wind gently ruffling the fronds of the palm trees over your head. You are close enough to the water to hear the waves gently lapping the edge of the beach. Run your fingers through the sand. It is so fine and white, smooth to the touch. It is warm on your hands. The waves are just touching your toes. Feel the cool, clear water as it washes over your toes and recedes again. You feel calm and relaxed, completely peaceful. You have been lying here for hours. You are so relaxed that you are almost asleep. The sun is beating down on you, warm and comforting. The breeze gently blows over you, keeping you cool. The waves gently tickle your toes. You are calm and relaxed.

2. Imagine that you are running through a field of flowers. Feel the wind in your hair as you run. You are jumping over small rocks. Feel the grass brushing against your legs as you pass. The sun is shining, warm and bright. The air smells like spring. You slow down and finally flop down on the grass, panting from your exhilarating run. Feel the soft grass against your face. Turn your head and smell the flowers. What colour are they? What do they smell like? See the butterfly go by? What colour is it? You hear birds singing from the trees near-by. What is their song? Touch the grass beside you. It is soft and clean and green. Pick a flower and smell it. Feel its velvety petals. Look up in the sky. See the soft white cloud drifting by? What does its shape remind you of? What does it look like? An animal? What kind? Here comes your puppy, running up to greet you. What colour is your puppy? Feel its wet little tongue as it licks your face. Run your fingers over its soft fluffy fur. Gather your puppy up into your arms and stand up. It's time to walk home.

3. Imagine that you are sitting in a forest. There are huge trees all around you. You are sitting on a rock that is covered in soft green moss. It's a very large rock. You can dangle your feet over the edge of the rock and they don't quite touch the

ground. In front of you is a fast-moving little stream. Listen to the sound of the water running over the little rocks in the stream. It sounds like the stream is singing. Listen to the birds singing in the tree branches over your head. Look up. The trees are enormous; they are so tall they form a canopy over your head. The wind is gently rustling the leaves. They, too, are singing. Everything is peaceful and calm. The only sounds you hear are the sounds of nature. Feel the moss on the rock you are sitting on. It feels cool and soft. Look at the pebbles in the stream. As the wind moves the leaves, the sun breaks through and glistens off of the pebbles in the stream. Look at their beautiful colours. The water looks so inviting. Jump down from your rock and walk towards the brook. Put your bare toes in the water. It is cool, but not cold. The water is crystal clear. You can see you toes on the bottom. Feel the water running over them. Feel the smoothness of the pebbles. Reach down and pick up a pretty stone. Put it in your pocket and step out of the brook. Climb up onto the bank. Feel the soft moss under your feet. It's time to walk home.

Variation #1. Instead of leading students to a certain location, invite students to picture an environment in which they feel calm, comfortable and safe. Ask them questions about what they see, hear, feel, taste and smell. Help them to bring the images alive for themselves.

POSITIVE IMAGINING

This has been used successfully by sports teams before big games, actors before a performance, or people facing an interview for a new job. It is a matter of imagining what you want to have happen, in order to put yourself in a positive frame of mind to allow for the outcome you seek. As part of a relaxation lesson, students can learn it as a technique to be used whenever they are in stressful situation. The leader can narrate them through a sample exercise, then ask the students to silently take themselves through a situation that they are worried about in their own lives.

Sample narration:

1. Imagine that you have a test next class. You have studied for it and know the material, but you are nervous and afraid that you will forget all of it as soon as you get your test paper. Imagine yourself turning over your test paper. You read the first question. It is something that you remember very well. Imagine yourself writing the correct answer. You read the next question. It too is easy to answer correctly. You are full of confidence as you continue to answer all of the questions. You feel calm and sure of yourself as you work your way through the test.

CIRCLE MASSAGE

This is a good exercise to both energize and relax the students at the beginning of a lesson. It also gets them involved in close contact group work very quickly in a non-threatening manner.

Method: Students stand in a circle. Everyone turns to their right and gently massages the neck and shoulders of the student in front of them. Remind students to only massage muscle mass, never bone (spine). It could include gentle tapping motions with a cupped hand and chopping motions with both hands brushing past each other very rapidly. Finish the massage with "The Whoosh," one firm down-stroke on each side of the spine, beginning at the shoulders and going down to the waist. This draws the last bit of tension away from the body. Turn and repeat the exercise with the student on the left.

BACK MASSAGE

Method: Students forms pairs, with one partner sitting cross-legged on the floor and the other kneeling behind him, gently massaging his neck, shoulders and back. It could include tapping and chopping motions on each side of the spine. It finishes with "The 'Whoosh," a single downward stroke with both hands to remove the final bit of tension.

NECK MASSAGE

Method: Students form pairs with one partner sitting cross-legged on the floor and the other partner lying on his back, resting his head on his partner's crossed legs. This cradles his head and puts it in a good position for an effective neck massage. His partner massages his neck and base of his skull, pulling his head gently towards herself, gently turning it from side to side. This is a great tension reliever for someone with a headache.

FOOT MASSAGE

They say that if your feet feel good, your whole body will feel good. While giving someone a thorough foot massage might accomplish just that, most young people will not feel comfortable giving each other a foot massage. However, they may enjoy performing this foot-to-foot massage.

Method: In pairs, one student lies face down on a towel or mat, with only socks on his feet. His partner stands facing his feet, in her socks, and slowly "walks" up his feet with her toes. As long as she keeps her heels on the floor, she won't hurt his feet, but will make them feel tingly and massaged.

tableaux
EXERCISES

A tableau can be described as frozen moment in time; a picture or a statue. Tableaux (plural) can be taught as an abstract concept, and then used for a wide variety of exercises.

Explanation to group: I want you all to mingle around in this room. Find your own paths, without making contact with anyone else. When I say "freeze" (or bang the tambourine or drum, or blow the whistle), I want you to stop short in whatever pose you're in at the time.

Method: Have the students repeat this several times, until they are accustomed to the idea of quickly coming to a complete stop. Then introduce different things to do or become when they freeze. Keep encouraging them to use their whole bodies, not just their faces.

The first time this game is played, call out the emotion, sport, occupation, etc. they are to freeze into for everyone to try. In later classes, this exercise can be repeated, having the students choose their own individual tableau within a category.

- Depicting an emotion—happy, sad, scared, excited, etc.

- Depicting a colour—this becomes an emotion—how does it feel to be blue, or yellow, or pink?

- Depicting a participant in a sport—baseball, fencing, swimming, etc.

- Depicting a person engaged in a certain occupation—doctor, teacher, wrestler, ballet dancer, truck driver, ditch digger, etc.

Or, as an alternate introduction to the concept of tableaux, the ALPHABET EXERCISE (see TABLEAUX PARTNER EXERCISES) can be played.

After exploring several of these exercises, it's time to explain what they've been doing:

Explanation to group: What we have been doing are tableaux. Tableau is a French word meaning picture. A tableau is a snapshot that you take during an activity that freezes the action for you to take a look at. It's a moment frozen in time. Sometimes we'll also talk about tableaux as being statues, something that you can form with your bodies. When I talk about a statue tableau, you need to be connected to the other people in your group in some way, as if you were formed out of one lump of clay, or all carved out of one rock. If I talk about a picture tableau, it's like any photograph, where the people are not necessarily physically connected, but are all part of the same photograph. Generally, abstract ideas or concepts are best shown by a statue tableau and a tableau that tells a story will need a photograph.

DESIGN CONCEPTS THROUGH TABLEAUX

Using pair and small group tableaux exercises is an effective way of teaching basic design elements, which will become important when they design tableaux to become part of the stage pictures they create for presentations.

Elements of design demonstrated through tableaux:

> Balance—literal and visual
> Symmetry and asymmetry—formal verses informal
> Line—static versus dynamic
> Mass—positive and negative space

BALANCE—Literal

Literal balance refers to students in a tableau supporting each other in some physical way.

Method: Working with a partner, have the students create a tableau in which:

- one student balances the other (dependent)

- both students need each other for balance (interdependent)

Have students show their tableaux and ask the group to identify some aspects that they have in common. What you will find is that most interdependent tableaux will be symmetrical, with one student in a mirror image pose of the other.

BALANCE—Visual

While literal balance can be discovered in an interdependent tableau, visual balance is another concept. It refers to the stage picture as a whole, what the audience sees. While much class work is focused on creating theatre as a means of self-expression and exploring a student's creativity, there may also be a place at some point for performing, even if only for each other, as in the GROUP PERFORMANCE exercises. In some cases, these exercises will involve tableaux, where visual balance is very important. Even if the scene is full of action, visual balance should always be considered.

The stage area can be viewed as a seesaw. If there is equal weight on both sides, it is balanced; therefore, when there are approximately the same number of people on each side of the stage, it will appear balanced. Set pieces also contribute weight to the stage and must be considered in the final stage picture. There are, of course, scenes in which the seesaw should be weighted to one side or the other. This could occur when the audience should see that someone is being overpowered (an employee sitting on a small chair and the boss behind a huge desk), or in danger (one person alone against a gang in a back alley).

Visual balance is simply one more thing that the group must consider, in order to have the audience understand what mood or meaning they are trying to convey.

NOTE: As a rehearsal tool, stage pictures can be assessed very quickly while rehearsing a scene by having the director call "freeze" at any time. The actors freeze in tableau and the director can see what the stage picture "reads"; what the audience will understand by the picture that has been created. All stage action is a huge series of tableaux. Each one should have a purpose and lead the audience in a direction that is consistent with the theme of the play.

SYMMETRY AND ASYMMETRY

Symmetry: repetition of exactly the same parts facing each other or the centre. The same on both sides.

Asymmetry: lack of symmetry. Different on each side.

- Have students explore non-symmetrical, or asymmetrical poses that are still interdependent.

- Have students form groups of six. Setting aside the dependent factor in the next tableaux, have all members of the group simply connected in some way, to:

    Form symmetrical tableaux.
    Form asymmetrical tableaux.

- Have students view other groups' tableaux and assess which ones they find most interesting. Guide them to discover that when a tableaux has more than one level, it creates interest for the viewer.

- Have students create new tableaus in which they consider using multilevel poses, having some students low to the floor, others at a medium height, and other as high as possible.

- Have students view other groups' tableaux and assess whether the tableau has a formal or informal, relaxed feeling to it. Guide them to discover that tableaux that are symmetrical tend to appear more formal, while an asymmetrical tableau will suggest an informal, casual feeling. Help the students explore what this means for future work by discovering when they would appropriately use a more formal tableau and when an asymmetrical pose would demonstrate what they were trying to portray:

- Have students create a posed portrait of a family that is very upper crust and proper, where family members don't communicate on anything but a formal level (symmetry will show this best).

- Have students create a posed family portrait of a rural family, who are casual, warm and relaxed with each other, having their picture taken outdoors (asymmetry will show this best).

LINE

- Have students discuss whether a symmetrical tableau or an asymmetrical tableau will be better able to convey the feeling of moment. Which one looks more likely to burst into action? Demonstrate this theory by asking the students to form tableaux of:

- A newspaper photograph of one head of government meeting another head of state from another country.

- A photograph taken at a baseball game as the batter going for a home run is struck out.

- Have students view each other's tableaux and discuss them in terms of dynamic action verses static non-action. Diagonal lines suggest movement. Horizontal and vertical lines appear more grounded and immobile. Multiple levels add interest to any tableau.

MASS

A person's body has mass. It can be seen and touched. It is, therefore, positive space. The area around a person can then be described as negative space.

- Have students explore how they can create shapes of negative space with their own bodies (one hand on a hip forms a tri-angle, etc.). They can also use the floor or a wall as positive space and create shapes in relationship to a flat surface. Then:

- Have students form groups of six. Each player takes a turn as the sculptor, moulding the rest of the group into a tableau that contains lots of large shapes of negative space. Once the creation is complete, the artist crawls through the sculpture, exploring the negative spaces.

Students' awareness of the design elements used in creating tableaux will assist them in making their tableaux more effective as they use them in future exercises. They will have an understanding of how best to have them portray an idea or relationship.

PARTNER TABLEAUX EXERCISES

THE ALPHABET

Method: Students work with their partners to create each letter of the alphabet. The leader specifies whether it should be upper or lower case.

Variation #1. Once letters are formed, the exercise can be further used as a physical warm-up, by having pairs recreate the tableaux quickly, in succession.

Variation #2. As a concentration exercise, the leader can call out letters at random, as pairs remember and recreate tableaux they used in the first exercise.

SCULPTURE GARDEN

Method: Students take turns creating a famous statue with their partners as their models. Once they have posed their statues, the other sculptors tour the statues, trying to identify them.

CLAYMOTION

Method: Students take turns moulding their partner's bodies into the expression of an emotion. Once they have completed the creation, other sculptors take a tour, trying to identify the emotions portrayed.

Variation #1. Once the class has advanced in their use of tableaux, repeat this exercise, having the statues come alive on command and vocalize their emotion.

Variation #2. Advanced work—Have a sculptor work with two models, creating an emotion with each statue's posture. On command, the statues come alive and improvise a scene in their character's prescribed emotional state.

TURN AND FREEZE

This can be used as an introduction to the concept of improvisation.

Method:

Step 1: Pairs turn their backs on each other. One partner moves in a random fashion, the other waits for a moment, then says "freeze," turns and studies the tableau his partner has made. Once he has decided what the pose has reminded him of, he thanks his partner, who returns to a neutral position. The exercise is repeated with reverse roles.

Step 2: The exercise is repeated with one partner saying one line of dialogue to the other, who is frozen, before roles are reversed.

Step 3: The exercise is repeated with the partners responding to the line of dialogue given.

Step 4: The exercise is repeated with the partners carrying on the dialogue for a minute, allowing the scene to develop.

FLUID TABLEAUX

Method: One partner creates an abstract tableau. Her partner creates a complementary tableau, fitting her body around some part of her partner's tableau, but not touching her. The first partner then breaks the tableau and creates a new one fitting into her partner's tableau. They continue to take turns reforming the tableau, until "time" is called.

Variation #1. This exercise can be done to music; with the students encouraged to move to the music while going from one posture to another. The style of the music will dictate the style of the movement. Various pieces of music could be used.

Variation #2. This exercise can also be done with trios, or small groups of four or five students, rather than pairs, with each person changing the tableau in turn.

POINT OF CONTACT

Method: Partners create a tableau with a specified number of contact points with the floor; e.g., two partners standing = four points of contact. Now find a tableau with only three points of contact with the floor, balancing each other. Number of points allowed to be feet can also be specified to make it more challenging. Move from pairs to groups of four, and then six, and repeat the exercise.

SMALL GROUP TABLEAUX EXERCISES

NAME THE TABLEAU

Method: Group stands in a circle. Each student has a turn at naming three people from the group who will enter the circle, and naming the tableau that they will form. The title may be an abstract concept, such as "friendship", or "utopia". Therefore, the statue tableaux will also be very abstract in nature. This exercise works best in a group of twelve to fifteen people. If the group is very large, make two circles in order to all have more turns and to maintain the interest in the exercise.

THEMES

Method: Groups form tableaux depicting a theme. All groups can form these simultaneously, or groups can come up with their own themes and have the whole group view them and guess the theme.

Sample themes: friendship, war, loss, love, the adventure, etc.

Variation #1. Instead of themes, groups can form family portraits. The family types can be picked from a deck of cards containing various possibilities; e.g., Circus family, short family, tall family, goofy family, intellectual family, mortician's family, ghost family, royal family, hillbilly family, explorer's family, etc.

Variation #2. Once a tableau has been formed, sounds can be added to create a soundscape of the theme. This can be done with a variety of themes, including a full range of subjects within themes, such as emotions (happy, sad, fearful, etc.), attitudes (love, hate, envy, etc.), environments (factory, stormy night, jungle, ocean, etc.).

Variation #3. Repetitive movements can be added to the sounds, to create a living, breathing entity on a theme.

HEADLINES

Tableaux can be created depicting photos from newspapers' front pages, real or imagined. Once the tableau is presented for the whole group, they can guess what the caption under the photo might say.

Variation #1. The tableau can come to life, with the group enacting what immediately followed the taking of the photo.

Variation #2. The group can enact the scene that preceded the taking of the photograph. The scene ends with all players in the position of their original tableaux.

Variation #3. Specify what kind of a publication the headline was part of in order to create different kinds of scenes.

Sample publications:

> Teen Magazine
> Daily Paper
> Supermarket Tabloid
> Woman's Magazine
> Sports Magazine
> Pet Lover's Weekly
> Travel Guide

LECTURE

Method: One student gives the whole group a lecture on a specific topic—real or silly. Four or five students work with him, creating tableaux that become the slide show, illustrating his lecture.

BEGINNING AND ENDING—see IMPROV WITH AN AUDIENCE

Other uses for tableaux—see STUDENT GROUP PROJECTS: Fairytale Theatre and Collage Collectives.

voice

voice
EXERCISES

While an introductory drama class may not be the place to develop a fully-trained stage voice, it is certainly appropriate to include some voice work. It's important for students to use their voices properly, working on breath control and voice projection in order to develop a stage voice without strain or damage to this important instrument.

VOICE PRODUCTION

Voice production can be broken down into four stages:

1. Respiration
2. Phonation
3. Resonation
4. Articulation

1. **Respiration:** This is the process by which air reaches the vocal folds. A well controlled voice begins in the diaphragm, the web-like membrane of muscle and sinew attached to the lower rib cage that separates the thorax from the abdomen. When air is expelled, the diaphragm slowly relaxes. As we inhale, the diaphragm contracts, pushing against the abdomen, raising the rib cage as air fills the lungs. As we exhale, the diaphragm can be used to control the flow of air, giving our voice support.

   Have students find their diaphragms by standing up straight and placing their fingertips on the bottom of their rib cages, and then drawing a line across their bodies. Have them place a hand on their stomachs covering this line, during the following exercises:

a) Say, "Ha, ha, ha, ha, ha." Feel the diaphragm jump and the hand move at each sound. This is the diaphragm working to push the air from the lungs. Have them repeat the sounds so that the hand doesn't jump against the stomach. This is a weak voice, unsupported by the diaphragm. Say, "Hello, how are you? Hurry up," and other phrases, feeling the diaphragm move.

b) Lie on the floor, facing the ceiling. Place a hand on the diaphragm, inhale to a count of twenty, and then exhale to the same count. Feel the diaphragm rise on the inhalations and lower on the exhalations. Release the air to the sound of AHH, as slowly as possible, finding a spot on the ceiling on which to focus the sound.

It is important to fill the lungs with air to insure sufficient breath to speak clearly. Raising shoulders, of course, does nothing to increase lung capacity.

2. **Phonation** is the passage of the air from the lungs, through the vibrating vocal folds within the larynx and out of the mouth and nose.

It is very important to relax the throat as the air passes through. There is a tendency to raise the pitch when trying to increase the volume, thereby tightening the vocal folds and causing the voice to strain. This is both unpleasant to listen to and damages the folds, leading to a sore, scratchy throat by the end of a performance.

a) Drop the head forward, releasing all tension in the neck. Let it drop from side to side. If dropping backward, it is important to open the mouth. Roll head from side to side. Avoid rolling through the back, as it tends to crunch the cartilage at the back of the neck.

b) Standing with feet shoulder-width apart, drop the head forward, followed by the shoulders and back, finally dropping forward from the waist, on an exhale. In this position, shake the head and shoulders to insure a total release of tension. Then slowly roll back up, one vertebra at a time, with the head being the last to fall back into place in an upright position. The inhale continues as the arms reach above the head. The exhale triggers a repetition of the exercise.

Variation #1. THE WHOOSH, see RELAXATION EXERCISES

3. **Resonation:** Without resonation, the sounds made by the vibrating vocal folds would scarcely be audible. The slight vibration of air in the back of the throat, mouth and sometimes the nose accentuate the sound already begun in the larynx. It is in these resonating chambers that sounds are selectively amplified to become the sounds we hear.

   The more open the resonating chambers, the stronger and clearer the sound. This is why a vowel sound carries better than a consonant.

   a) Have students open their mouths wide and yawn, the ultimate throat-relaxing exercise. Now, keeping that same open feeling in the throat, release a slow sustained AHH sound.

   b) Starting at a mid-range, comfortable pitch, perform this exercise using all of the vowel sounds, rising one note with each repetition: A-E-I-O-U. Hold each sound for a moment before going on to the next. Maintain an open throat as the pitch rises.

Variation #1. Instead of simple vowel sounds, repeat the sounds:

"UN GA YA YA LA LA MA MA."

4. **Articulation:** The vibrating air in the resonating chambers is modified by the tongue, lips, teeth, soft palate and jaw to become the sounds that we recognize as words. There are many articulation drills, such as tongue twisters, to encourage the proper use of these tools in forming words clearly.

   a) Peanut butter. Pretend to have a mouthful of peanut butter. Use the tongue to clear it out of first one cheek, then the other and finally, around the front of the teeth.

   b) Relax the lips and allow them to vibrate, blowing air out on a BRRRRR sound. Now allow the tongue to relax and vibrate,

RRRRRR. Add the letter B to produce the sounds BREEEEE and BRAAAA, smiling widely.

c) Smile widely and produce the sound SSSSSSS. Purse the lips to create the sound SHHHHH. Go from one to the other quickly.

d) Say the alphabet as quickly and clearly as possible. As a breath control exercise, repeat the alphabet three times in one breath.

e) Keeping the jaw and neck relaxed, repeat these tongue twisters as many times as possible in one breath. Keep the volume and strength of the voice constant until the end of the breath.

> The lips, the teeth, the tip of the tongue.
> Toy boat.
> Lemon liniment.
> She sells seashells at the sea shore.

BREATH CONTROL

Along with learning how to articulate words comes control of the breath, using only as much at one time as is needed. The sound produced should be as strong at the end of the phrase as it is at the beginning.

1. Repeat each line five times in one breath.

a) Round and round
   Round and round the rugged rock
   Round and round the rugged rock the ragged rascal ran

b) Bring the butter
   Bring the butter to the baker
   Bring the butter to the baker to be baked
   Bring the butter to the baker to be baked into the bread

c) Sit with Shelly
   Sit with Shelly and Sammy
   Sit with Shelly and Sammy Smithers
   Sit with Shelly and Sammy Smithers and slip
   Sit with Shelly and Sammy Smithers and slip some salt into
      their soup

d) Did you drag
Did you drag the Dalmatian
Did you drag the Dalmatian to the den
Did you drag the Dalmatian to the den with the dragons
Did you drag the Dalmatian to the den with the dragons
  dancing
Did you drag the Dalmatian to the den with the dragons
  dancing dumbly in the dark

2. Limericks can be used in the same way, slowly for articulation, and quickly for breath control. Try to use only one breath per limerick.

a) There was a young lady of Niger,
   Who smiled as she rode on a tiger.
   They returned from the ride with the lady inside
   and a smile on the face of the tiger.

b) There was an old man with a beard,
   who said, "It is just as I feared,
   two owls and a hen,
   four larks and a wren
   have just built a home in my beard."

c) There was a young man of Japan,
   wrote verses that no one could scan.
   When they told him 'twas so,
   He replied, "Yes, I know,
   But I like to get as many words in the last line as
   I possibly can."

d) There was a young man of Quebec
   who stood in the snow to his neck.
   When they said, "Are you frizz?"
   He replied, "Yes, I is,
   but we don't call this cold in Quebec."

e) There was a an old man of Nantucket,
   who kept all of his gold in a bucket,
   till his daughter named Nan
   ran away with a man,
   and as for the bucket, Nantucket.

f) There was a young fellow named Dave
   whose parents told him to behave.
   But he played his guitar
   in a style most bizarre
   and created an outlandish new wave.

g) There was an young lady named Loni
   Whose skin was a deep shade of tawny.
   Till her mother said, "Come and get out of the sun.
   You're prettier when you are bonny."

3. Repeat the following excerpt from Gilbert and Sullivan's *The Mikado*. Try to keep the articulation very clean and say the entire passage in one breath.

> To sit in sullen silence in a dull, dark dock
> In a pestilential prison with a life-long lock
> Awaiting the sensation of a short sharp shock
> From a cheap and chippy chopper on a big black block.

ELEMENTS OF EFFECTIVE SPEECH

After working on breath control and articulation, there are other elements of speech that can be focused on to improve the quality of a stage voice. It is not enough for the voice simply to be heard. In order to keep the listener interested in the words, the voice must not be monotonous and boring. It must have variety. This may be achieved by the speaker simply being interested in what he is saying and conveying this to his audience, but there are also technical ways of bringing variety to the voice. This is achieved by varying:

1. Pitch
2. Emphasis
3. Tone
4. Tempo/pauses
5. Volume
6. Rhythm

1. **Pitch** refers to the highs and lows of the voice. The speaker should stay within a comfortable range, in order to sound natural. Pitch will vary naturally if the speaker follows the intent of a word or phrase.

a) Repeat the following words and phrases aloud, reflecting the intention in brackets:

Hello	(Do I know you?)
Hello	(I haven't seen you in ages)
Hello	(Thank God I haven't seen you in ages)
Hello	(I can't believe that you didn't get that joke)
Do you really think so?	(I don't know what to do)
Do you really think so?	(I am so glad you agree)
Do you really think so?	(I certainly don't)
Do you really think so?	(I just want you to be sure)
I'm leaving now	(I love you and I'll be right back)
I'm leaving now	(And I don't ever want to come back)
I'm leaving now	(Because you hurt my feelings)
I'm leaving now	(I'm pretending to leave so I can eavesdrop)
May I have that?	(It's mine and you took it)
May I have that?	(I can't believe you'd let me keep it)
May I have that?	(I can't believe you were giving it to HER)
May I have that?	(It's ugly and I don't really want it)

b) Use the alphabet to:

1. Give a speech. Saying only the letters of the alphabet, let the real text play in your head. Chose a topic you feel passionate about: e.g., your favorite piece of music. The saddest movie you ever saw. The most fun you ever had on a vacation.

2. Hold a conversation between partners. Use only the alphabet. One person picks up the next letter when it's his turn to speak; e.g., talk about the weather. Bring up the money your friend owes you. Decide which movie to go and see. Have a pointless argument.

2. **Emphasis** is finding the important words in a sentence to stress to convey meaning and intent or to create interest.

a) Read this paragraph, making its meaning absolutely clear:

I will go to see Will, if you will come with me. Will will make us dinner, if we will bring Will the dessert. Will will read his Uncle William's will after dinner.

b) When reading Shakespeare, it is always important to emphasis those words which will bring out the meaning of his words most clearly:

As You Like It—Act III, scene 5

Phoebe:
I would not be thy executioner,
I fly thee, for I would not injure thee:
Thou tell'st me there is murder in mine eye;
Tis pretty, sure, and very probable,
That eyes, that are the frail'st and the softest things,
Who shut their coward gates on atomies,
Should be call'd tyrants, butchers, murderers!
Now I do frown on thee with all my heart,
And if mine eyes can wound, why now let them kill thee,
Now counterfeit to swoon, why now fall down,
Or if thou canst not, O, for shame, for shame,
Lie not, to say mine eyes are murderers!
Now show the wound mine eyes hath made in thee,
Scratch thee but with a pin, and there remains
Some scar of it; lean upon a rush,
The cicatrice and capable impressure
Thy palm some moment keeps; but now mine eyes,
Which I have darted at thee, hurt thee not,
Nor, I am sure, there is no force in eyes that can do hurt.

If using emphasis to create interest, choose to emphasize the words that will catch the listener's ear and help you to create a mood or draw a picture with your words.

c) Read this poem, choosing words to emphasis in order to paint the picture of the scene described by the poet. Play with drawing out long vowel sounds. Of course, the other elements of speech—pitch, tone, tempo and volume—will also make the reading of this poem more effective.

Daffodils
  by William Wordsworth

I wandered lonely as a cloud
    That floats on high o'er vales and hills,
When all at once I saw a crowd,
    A host, of golden Daffodils;
Beside the lake, beneath the trees,
Fluttering and dancing in the breeze.

Continuous as the stars that shine
    And twinkle on the Milky Way,
They stretched in never-ending line
    Along the margin of the bay:
Ten thousand saw I at a glance,
Tossing their heads in sprightly dance.

The waves beside them danced; but they
    Out-did the sparkling waves with glee:
A poet could not but be gay,
    In such a jocund company:
I gazed—and gazed—but little thought
What wealth the show to me had brought:

For oft, when on my couch I lie
    In vacant or in pensive mood,
They flash upon that inward eye
    Which is the bliss of solitude;
And then my heart with pleasure fills,
And dances with the Daffodils.

3. **Tone** refers to the mood the speaker wishes to create for the listener. The tone will dictate whether his voice will be dark or light. This is best discovered by deciding what the author's attitude is towards the material.

a) Read this poem, deciding what the speaker's attitude is in each stanza. This poem makes use of repetition. When a word or phrase is repeated, such as the line, "I can't see what he sees in her," find a new attitude for each of the lines. Bringing this attitude out in the line delivery will vary the lines' presentation. This will likely mean that a different word is emphasized in each repetition.

I Can't Think What He Sees In Her
by A.P. Herbert

Jealousy's an awful thing and foreign to my nature:
I'd punish it by law if I was in the Legislature.
One can't have all of anyone, and wanting it is mean,
But still, there is a limit, and I speak of Miss Duveen.

    I'm not a jealous woman,
        But I can't see what he sees in her,
            I can't see what he sees in her,
                I can't see what he sees in her!

    If she was something striking
    I could understand the liking,
And I wouldn't have a word to say to that:
    But I can't see why he's fond
    Of that objectionable blonde—
That fluffy little, stuffy little, flashy little, trashy little,
    creepy-crawly, music-hally, horrid little CAT!

I wouldn't say a word against the girl—be sure of that;
It's not the creature's fault she has the manners of a rat.
Her dresses may be dowdy, but her hair is always new,
And if she squints a little bit—well, many people do.

I'm not a jealous woman,
>But I can't see what he sees in her,
>>I can't see what he sees in her,
>>>I can't see what he sees in her!

He's absolutely free—
There's no bitterness in me,
Through an ordinary woman would explode:
>I'd only like to know
>What he sees in such a crow,
As that insinuating, calculating, irritating, titivating,
>sleepy little, creepy little, sticky little TOAD.

4. **Tempo/pauses.** When the tempo is varied, the interest of the audience is maintained. It also varies according to the mood of the piece. A pause before a word heightens its importance; a pause after a word or phrase gives the audience time to ponder its significance.

a) Read the following paragraphs, pausing where appropriate, for effect:

Always remember—if you want people to realize the importance of the words you are saying, you cannot spit them all out at the same time. You must take all the time their importance requires. Sometimes, it may be necessary to even stop...and wait for your audience to grasp the meaning of your words.

You may also use pauses for dramatic effect. When you know that something is out there in the black night, you want to pause, because you don't want your listener to find out too quickly what it is. You'll want to speak slowly to build suspense. But then—once you have revealed that you are being chased by the world's largest living monster, you may want to speak very fast, in short choppy sentences, every breath coming out in short little gasps, to indicate to your audience just how frightened you really are.

5. **Volume.** The voice will naturally increase in volume to emphatically make a point and soften to create a warm loving mood. The volume of the voice must also be appropriate for the size of the audience and the distance it is away from the speaker.

a) Repeat the following sentences twice, the first time in anger, the second time in a warm welcoming tone.

> Take that thing out of the box.
> I told you that I would be coming at 4:00.
> You always say stuff like that.
> Come over here right now.
> I can't help feeling like that.
> What do you want me to say?
> I can't believe you said that.

b) Place a student five steps away from the group. Have the speaker repeat a limerick, give instructions on making his favourite sandwich—or deliver any material he is familiar with. Instruct him to speak loudly enough for the group to hear him comfortably. After a few sentences, have him move away from the group another five steps and continue speaking. Repeat this process until he is as far away from the group as the space will allow. His volume should increase to accommodate the distance that he is from his audience.

6. **Rhythm.** When reading a piece of pose, or free-form verse, the reader decides on the rhythm he will adopt. If he wishes to relax his audience, his tone will be soothing and his rhythm fairly regular, with few changes to jolt his audience from being lulled into a dream-like state. However, if it is his intent to shock, motivate, inspire or excite his audience, his rhythm will go through many changes, constantly challenging his audience to keep up with him. This, of course, relates also to volume, pauses and tempo—all of which, when varied, will keep his voice from falling into a steady, even rhythm. There is another facet of rhythm when reading poetry, however, that needs to be addressed. Many pieces of classical poetry and modern poems, especially those written

for children, are written in an iambic pentameter rhythm. This means that every other syllable is accented. To read an iambic pentameter poem with an emphasis on every other syllable is death to the reading. The previous five ways of creating interest in a reading will be completely lost. The audience will not hear the words, they will simply hear the cadence of the rhythm. Utmost care must be taken to focus on those five factors of an effective reading. The meter of the poem must be disregarded completely. It will always be there in the background at any rate, but it cannot take over and become the only thing heard.

The first step in ignoring this rhythm is to look at the punctuation of the piece, rather than stopping at the end of every line whether the thought continues on to the next line or not. Significant pauses are only taken at a period, or in the middle of a line if needed for effect or emphasis. Then pitch, tone, tempo and volume can be explored and applied to the poem. Emphasis is especially important to accent words that are significant to the meaning of the poem and to create interest, regardless of their position in the line.

The following poem has been written in iambic pentameter. Read it aloud, trying not to fall into its rhythm.

Progress
by Alfred Lord Tennyson

As we surpass our fathers' skill,
    Our sons will shame our own;
A thousand things are hidden still,
    And not a hundred known.

And had some prophet spoken true
    Of all we shall achieve,
The wonders were so wildly new,
    That no man would believe.

Meanwhile, my brothers, work, and wield
    The forces of to-day,

And plough the Present like a field,
    And garner all you may!

You, what the cultured surface grows,
    Dispense with careful hands;
Deep under deep for ever goes,
    Heaven our heaven expands.

Of course, there may be times when the rhythm of a poem is stressed very effectively, probably only for short intervals, as a contrast to the rest of the poem, where it is not stressed. In other applications, such as poetry with a rap beat, it would be appropriate to maintain the intended rhythm of a poem.

POETRY

Poems are useful in demonstrating the techniques needed in developing one's voice; however, performing poetry has certainly lost popularity as an art form. In performing a piece of Reader's Theatre or Collage Collective poetry will play a vital role, but in all other areas of drama it will be largely forgotten. It does have a place, however, in acting as a bridge between speech work and drama. While students may not get very excited about the idea of choral speaking—collectively reciting a poem—they will undoubtedly enjoy poetry that lends itself to action.

The following poem is fun for any age group to work on. It could be done as a choral speech choir, with the lines divided between individual, small group and unison voices. However, the poem could really come alive with pantomime. Students pantomime the action of the poem, creating the monster with their bodies as well as their voices.

Jabberwocky
    from *Through the Looking-Glass*
      by Lewis Carroll

'Twas brillig, and the slithy toves
    Did gyre and gimble in the wabe:
All mimsy were the borogoves,

And the mome raths outgrabe.

'Beware the Jabberwock, my son!
    The jaws that bite, the claws that catch!
Beware the Jubjub bird, and shun
    The frumious Bandersnatch!'

He took his vorpal sword in hand:
    Long time the manxome foe he sought—
So rested he by the Tumtum tree,
    And stood awhile in thought.

And as in uffish thought he stood,
    The Jabberwock, with eyes of flame,
Came whiffling through the tulgey wood,
    And burbled as it came!

One, two! One two! And through and through
    The vorpal blade went snicker-snack!
He left it dead, and with its head
    He went galumphing back.

'And hast thou slain the Jabberwock?
    Come to my arms, my beamish boy!
O frabjous day! Callooh! Callay!'
    He chortled in his joy.

'Twas brillig, and the slithy toves
    Did gyre and gimble in the wabe:
All mimsy were the borogoves,
    And the mome raths outgrabe.

LITANY

Poetry can flow very naturally into litany, which can, in turn
introduce the concept of rituals. This would lead the group to
the project on creating an ancient ritual. The rhythms and
repetition of this invocation are a suitable introduction to ritual.

A LITANY FOR THE MOON

Leader:	Response:
Great Spirit of the night, hear our cry	Hear our cry
Oh moon, rise, rise up on high	Let it rise up
Fill the darkness with your light	Let it rise up
Great Spirit of the night, hear our cry	Hear our cry
Rise up in your fullness	Let it rise up
Gather the stars in the heavens	Gather them up
Bring forth the beasts for our hunt	Bring them forth
Let them be seen in the night	Let them be seen
Give us strength for the hunt	Give us strength
Guide our path in this journey	Guide our path
Oh moon, rise, rise up on high	Let it rise up
Great Spirit of the night, hear our cry	Hear our cry
Hear our cry	Hear our cry

Method: Divide the group into smaller groups of six or seven students. They are given ten to fifteen minutes to plan and rehearse how this litany will be performed. Movement patterns could be incorporated, as well as simple instruments to create a repetitive rhythm.

improvisation
EXERCISES

Improvisation is the act of creating a scene spontaneously, without preplanning. It is certainly a part of most exercises, however, the following exercises have improvisation as their main focus. These are the exercises that the class has warmed up to play. It may be several lessons into a session before they are ready to be introduced to the idea of improvisation, or "improv." When they are comfortable with the exercises and each other, they will go from doing partner exercises simultaneously to watching each other "perform."

RULES OF IMPROV

While advanced students may work without guidelines in a free-form improv, it is a good idea to introduce rules of improv to beginning students of drama. They will experience more success with their scenes if they follow these simple rules. They will also find that fellow students enjoy improvising with them, which is its own reward:

1. No blocking. The word blocking here refers to not accepting suggestions as they are given; e.g., partner A: "I sure hate getting wet in this downpour." Partner B: "It isn't raining." When a player blocks an idea given, it puts the other player in the position of defending the suggestion or coming up with a new one. Either way, it isn't fair to the player and doesn't allow the scene to move forward.

2. The first player to speak must give something to his partner, by answering either the who, what, where, when, or why of the scene they are going to build together.

3. Commit to your first idea. Don't second-guess yourself or try to plan what will happen next. Your first idea is usually your best one. Go with it and believe in it one hundred percent.

OBJECTIVES AND STRATEGIES

In every scene, whether it is scripted or improvised, each character has an objective, something that they want from the other character. This is their reason for being on the stage. If the characters don't want something from each other, the scene will die. Each character will use strategies to get what they want. In improvs, actors need to recognize when a strategy isn't working and move on to another one. The scene is over when one character gets what they want from the other, or both have reached an impasse. As a rule of thumb, an improv should have a clear objective for each character and each character should try three different strategies before calling an improv over. One of these strategies should be non-verbal, something that they DO to get what they want. The following exercise with a chair is a simple way to introduce the idea of objectives and strategies.

THE CHAIR

The exercise will teach students how to use strategies to met their objectives.

Method: One of the partners is sitting on a chair. The other is told to do whatever it takes to get the chair away from her partner, but WITHOUT PHYSICAL CONTACT. A discussion follows the exercise, after each partner has had a turn in each role. What did they do to get the chair? Did they try something else when the first thing didn't work? Did they finally get the chair? How, what did they say or do? Some verbal strategies could be to beg, threaten, offer a deal, or show need (advanced pregnancy, broken leg). Non-verbal strategies could include crying or fainting.

CONFLICT VERSUS HARMONY

Eventual harmony can provide an ending for a scene, but it's very difficult to make a scene interesting without conflict. While having two characters share the same objective and agree on the same strategies needed to achieve it would result in a great relationship, it makes for boring theatre, not to mention a very short scene. All theatre needs tension. This is generally brought about by characters having conflicting objectives. In scenarios with an outside source of tension, say an approaching avalanche, the scene will still not be very interesting unless the characters don't agree on the strategies needed to save themselves.

PARTNER IMPROVISATIONS

In the first stages of teaching improv, it's good to have students working simultaneously, with a partner. Not only does this provide a non-threatening environment where no one feels they are being watched and judged, it also means that no one has to wait for their turn to "play." In a little while they will be ready to watch each other, but the partner work still provides a good warm-up for the performance style of improvs.

LET'S

This exercise helps students experience rule #1: don't block.

Method: In pairs, students take turns making suggestions, which both partners immediately follow; e.g., "Let's go swimming." They mime going for a swim. The other partner says, "Let's brush our hair." Both partners brush their hair.

THIS IS FOR YOU

This is an exercise that gives students a starting point for an improv. It also demonstrates rule #3: Trust your first idea.

Method: Students work in pairs, taking turns giving each other a gift. The giver does not indicate size or weight of the imaginary gift. It is up to the receiver, upon opening the gift, to determine what it is. Appropriate dialogue accompanies the scene. Encourage students to trust themselves. A gift will appear as soon as they reach into the box.

Variation #1. A student reaches into his pocket and pulls out an imaginary object to share with his partner.

Variation #2. Partners walk to another area of the room and find an imaginary object on the floor. A scene begins at its discovery.

LET'S WORK IT OUT

This exercise allows students to develop their powers of persuasion, something they need while playing their strategies in order to meet their objectives in an improvised scene.

Method: Pairs are told that they have just won a trip anywhere in the world. The catch is that they must decide where to go, as they both must go to the same destination.

Variation #1. Pairs receive one million dollars. Both students must agree on how it is spent.

Variation #2. Pairs will receive a pet. They must agree on what kind.

TAG TEAM ARGUMENT

Method: The group is divided into smaller groups of six or eight students. Two students from each group begin an argument. On the leader's command of "Subs in," two other students from their group replace them, continuing the same argument.

PICK AN "A"

These exercises give students the parameters of their improvs—the set-up. Generally, the leader provides the who, what, where and when of a scene. Students begin the improv, working out the why.

INSTANT SCENARIOS

Method: Students are placed in pairs and asked to pick a player to become "A". The other player is "B". The leader provides them with characters and a situation, they improv the scene for a minute or two. The leader calls out that it is over, asks them to switch partners (see PARTNER WARM-UPS for ways to switch) and gives them a new scenario. They may reverse their roles and play the scene again before switching partners. A discussion on how they played it and how the roles felt could follow each scene.

Sample scenarios:

> A parent (or babysitter) with a child who doesn't want to eat her dinner, go to school, go to bed, pick up her toys, etc.
>
> A parent with a teenager sneaking in after curfew.
>
> A teacher with a student caught cheating on an exam.
>
> A store clerk with a shoplifter.
>
> A parent asking a teenager to baby-sit bratty children.
>
> A teenager who wants to borrow a car from an older sibling.
>
> A teenager who wants his/her friend to ask a girl/boy if she/he likes him.
>
> A policeman and a driver caught speeding.
>
> A night watchman and a thief.
>
> A nurse and a patient who wants to leave the hospital.
>
> Two bank robbers planning a break-in.
>
> A friend giving another friend some bad news.
>
> Two sisters/brothers who both want to use the same object.
>
> Two friends, shopping, who want to buy the same object/clothing.

NOTE: Conflict is more theatrically interesting than harmony, and more fun to play.

SALES PERSON

Method: Partners take turns trying to sell something to each other.

Sample sales: A three-legged horse.

A blind donkey.

A car with no wheels.

This room.

Swampland in Florida.

A trip on a home-made space ship.

A treasure map.

A raffle ticket.

ENTER ON CUE

Method: The leader provides partner "A" with a role, but not "B". It is "A's" job to enter the scene and provide "B" with enough information on the first line of dialogue for her to be able to figure out who she is and what is happening. This experience develops rule#2: Give your partner something.

Sample A roles: A tourist asking for directions.

A door to door salesperson.

A train passenger who has lost his/her ticket.

A sibling trying to borrow on next week's allowance.

A customer trying to find the right item in a store.

A customer trying to return an unwanted item.

FIRST LINE

Method: The leader provides partner A with the first line of dialogue. It provides the intent of the scene, but the actors fill in the information as to who they are and what is happening.

Sample lines: Let's get out of here.

I told you not to do that.

Why did we ever come in here?

What have you got behind your back?

She said that I could take it.

What am I going to wear?

How dare you call him that?

CHANGE OF AGE

Method: The leader provides the actors with an activity and with the characters involved in the activity, making both play peers, of the same age. After a few minutes, the leader calls out to continue the activity, but as different characters of a different age. Once each scene has been established, the leader can call out for them to switch back and forth. The activity always remains the same; the characters and their relationship to the activity changes. This also works well in small groups of three or four students.

Sample activities: Playing in the sandbox

- as five-year-olds in kindergarten
- as teens asked to build a sculpture
- as seniors in a home, sand therapy

Making a sandwich

- as five-year-olds
- as teens late for school
- as wealthy middle-aged people whose maid just quit
- as seniors on a picnic

Walking in the park

- as five-year-olds who are lost
- as teens skipping school
- as middle-aged people out for exercise
- as seniors walking their dogs

Cleaning house

- as five-year-olds, picking up toys
- as teen siblings—parents are away
- as adults, getting ready for yard sale
- as seniors, packing up memories

CONDITIONS

Method: Pairs are provided with an activity that remains constant throughout the scene, but the leader shouts out changes to the conditions while the scene is in progress. The partners must accommodate the changes and carry on with the scene.

Sample activities and changes:

Bathing a dog

- the dog becomes as big as a horse
- the bathwater turns into pudding
- the dog won't stay awake

Teaching a child to tie shoes

- the laces are ten feet long
- the laces are full of knots
- the shoes and laces are very muddy

Washing a car

- the car begins to roll away
- the car turns into a large truck
- the water hose has a great deal of pressure

Playing miniature golf

- the clubs shrink to one foot long
- the clubs weigh 50 lbs. each
- it starts to rain

Cleaning the house

- the ceiling drops to five feet off the floor
- the floor is tilted at a 30-degree angle
- the house catches on fire

Variation #1. Instead of the conditions changing in the scene's environment, the leader calls out changes to the condition of the characters themselves.

Sample scenes and changes:

Friends playing a game of golf

- Partner "A"—grows an extra arm
- Partner "B"—teeth become fangs

Siblings clean the house after a party

- Partner "A"—can't move his right leg
- partner "B"—shrinks to two feet tall

Parent/teenager eating at a restaurant

- Partner "A" gains 100 lbs.
- Partner "B" can't stop sneezing

TURN AND FREEZE—see TABLEAUX, partner exercises.

This exercise provides a new improv every time and is excellent for developing the skill of spontaneity—coming up with new ideas and not being afraid to go with them. (see third rule of improv)

Method: In pairs, students take turns beginning an improv based on the physical posture of their partners. For beginners and as fast warm-ups, the leader controls the length of the improv, telling students when to begin another and when to switch partners. For more advanced actors, the leader asks them to bring the improv to a logical conclusion (working on how to end an improv) and begin another at their own pace, with the same partner.

NOTE: In the latter scenario, students are being asked to consider how to know when an improv is over. Did it end with a flourish or simply die from lack of ideas?

THE QUEST

Method: Pairs of students link arms and narrate themselves through an adventure, with each student providing only one word of narration at a time. They alternate words as they pantomime the action of the story they are creating. This may or may not lead to a performance for the whole group. The theme of the adventure is set by a volunteer in the group providing an object, a geographical location and an occupation. The adventure then becomes a quest for the object, to the geographical location, carried out by two characters sharing the same occupation. All pairs work on the same adventure simultaneously.

IMPROVISATIONS WITH AN AUDIENCE

TAG TEAM IMPROVS

While watching each other improvise, these exercises are still non-threatening, because everyone gets a turn to play in quick succession to the rest of the group.

Method: Students sit in a circle with two players in the centre, who begin pairs improv with a turn and freeze exercise. At a physically interesting point in the improv, someone on the outside of the circle calls " freeze." The players freeze in tableau and the caller enters the circle and taps one of the players on the shoulder. That player sits down and the caller takes his place in the tableau, unfreezing and beginning an entirely new scene based on his tableau. The scene continues until someone else calls out for the players to freeze. The new caller begins a new scene. If this exercise is new for the group, the leader may choose to call freeze and send in the next person, insuring that everyone in the circle has a turn.

Variation #1. An object (prop) could be used in the scene. When an outside caller says "freeze," he comes into the centre and takes the object from the player holding it. In doing so, he transforms it into something else and begins a new scene.

Variation #2. The group forms two lines. The first person in each line begin an improv. The leader calls for them to freeze and sends in the next player from one line, who takes his teammate's position in the tableau. He begins a new scene. On the next call for them to freeze, the first person in the other line begins the next improv. In this way, each person plays two improvs: one in which the other person begins and one which she begins. This works well as a warm-up for other, more involved improv work.

Variation #3. Instead of replacing one of the players, the student who calls freeze starts a new scene based on the tableau of the first two. All three play the new scene. A fourth and fifth person could be added. The leader could then call freeze and have the fifth person leave. The four players left go back to the scene with four, and so on until only the original two players again continue their scene. In an advanced class, the leader could call out a number and return to the scene that contained that number of players, who would pick up where they left off in the appropriate scene number called in random order.

PAIR IMPROVS

In the following improvs, pairs of students are given the premise of the scene and improvise it for the whole group.

PUPPETS

Premise: Pairs are given a location and a relationship. Example: Two truck drivers in a coffee shop. They can speak, but they can't move. Each of them has a "puppet-handler" who moves them into position as they play the scene.

Variation #1. The actors can move, but off-stage voices provide the dialogue. They must make their actions match whatever the voices say they are doing.

FEATURES

Premise: Player B leaves the room while the group decides what his special feature will be. He returns and player A plays the scene, subtly giving him hints about his feature by the way in which she treats and responds to him.

Sample features: His nose is three feet long. He has an extra arm or leg, or a short tail. He has a long beard, or no hair at all. He is very short or very tall, etc.

Variation #1. As in the group warm-up exercise of YOU'RE FAMOUS, player B comes into the scene and tries to ascertain which famous person he is. Once he thinks he knows, he plays along, finding an ending to the scene in character.

Variation #2. Instead of a famous person, player B must figure out what his occupation, or physiological problem, attitude or mental state is.

ONE WORD ONLY

Premise: Players are given a location and must advance the plot of the scene using only one-word sentences.

Variation #1. Even more challenging. Players can say only one word, which follows the alphabet. Player A says a word beginning with A, player B says a word beginning with B, followed by A with a C-word and so on until the scene ends with a Z-word. Or, player A says any word of his choice. Player B must respond with a word beginning with the following letter. The players go right through the alphabet and continue with an A-word, finishing the scene when they arrive back at the letter that player A began the scene with.

Variation #2. Scene is played with only two- to four-word sentences.

Variation #3. Scene is played with players rhyming their responses with the last statement made by the other player.

SHOULD HAVE SAID

Premise: Players A and B are given a location and relationship to each other. Example: Two teens on a date in a movie theatre. Each player has an alter ego standing off to the side, who can say, "Should have said," at any time during the scene. When they do so, their player must say the opposite of their last line of dialogue. The other player responds to this new line and the scene continues.

I LOVE YOU

Premise: The players are given a location and situation. Example: Returning an unsuitable item at a store. The scene ends when one player finds a logical opportunity to say, "I love you."

Variation #1. Instead of the line, "I love you," the scene ends when one character can say whatever line was provided by the audience before the improv began.

EXPERT

Premise: One player is a talk show host. The other is the guest, who is given a field of expertise on which to be interviewed. Example: The life of the dung beetle. However, both players sit with their hands in their laps, while someone else sits behind them in another chair, with their arms through the sleeves of a jacket, which is draped over the front player. In this way, the front player does the character's voice, but the back player does the character's arms. Objects are placed on a table between the front players for the arms to use as props. The front players must incorporate their use into the dialogue.

Variation #1. Players stand at a table. The front players put their hands into shoes and lean their elbows on the table. They do the voice and the legs of this very short character, while the back player does the arms.

HE SAID/SHE SAID

Premise: Players A and B are given a location and relationship. Example: a teacher and student meet at a beach. As they play the scene, each has a narrator off to the side, providing the directions that the players must follow. Example: Player A— "Hi." Narrator—"she says as she picks up a handful of sand."

TRANSFER EMOTIONS

Premise: Players are given a location and an emotion. Example: At a bank. Player A is happy, player B is worried. As the scene progresses, the players must switch emotions.

HIDDEN OBJECTIVE

Premise: Each player is told secretly what he or she wants from the other player. Example: Player A wants player B's watch. Player B wants player A to say she loves her mother. The scene ends when one player gets what she wants.

NO QUESTIONS ASKED

Premise: Players are given a location. Example: A rock concert. Neither player is allowed to ask a question. The first player to ask a question "loses" the improv and it ends.

GET THE HAT

Premise: The players are given a relationship. Example: Brothers. Each player wears a hat. The scene is over when one player removes the hat of the other. This must be done without turning the improv into a scene about stealing hats. The topic of conversation is about anything else but the hat. They try to catch the other player off guard and snatch the hat. The players can protect their hats, but not guard them by touching them, carrying them, hiding them, etc.

PHYSICAL CONTACT

Premise: Players cannot speak to each other unless they are touching. Once given a location, they must play a scene and find realistic reasons to touch in order to be able to speak. If they solve the problem by becoming, for example, mother and child and hold hands, the contact must be broken, as the rule is that a new contact must be made for each time a player speaks.

UNLIKELY COMBINATIONS

Premise: Players create a scene with suggestions received by picking a card from each of three decks. One deck contains occupations, another locations and the last, objects. Both characters become the same occupation. So, for example, they could be asked to play a scene as:

> Two nuns in a rowboat with a vacuum cleaner.
> Two hairdressers in the park with a banana.

With a good selection in each deck, the combinations are endless.

BEGINNING AND ENDING

Premise: Players are given a beginning tableau and an ending tableau by a volunteer from the audience. They begin a scene based on the first tableau. The scene is over when the scene flows naturally into the ending tableau.

MOVIE

Premise: Players are given characters and a location. A director stands off to the side and shouts instructions at random that the characters must react to.

Sample directions: Slow motion, rewind, fast forward, freeze-frame, pause, play.

PLAY IT BACKWARDS

Premise: Players play an entire scene backwards, beginning with the ending. The first word could be good-bye. The scene ends with a hello. This is actually quite difficult to do and may be tried first as a pair improv, with no audience.

FOREIGN FLICK

Premise: Players play an action scene in gibberish. Each player has a translator off to the side to translate each line into English.

Variation #1. Dubbing. Players perform the scene in pantomime, moving their lips, with their partners off to the sides dubbing in their lines of dialogue.

ENTER ON CUE—see PARTNER IMPROVS

Variation #1. Instead of having B enter, try to figure out who he is and finish the scene, as soon as B figures out who he is he must find a way to leave the scene within the context of the dialogue that has been established.

LEAVE SOMETHING BEHIND

Premise: Players are given characters and a location. Example: a mother and daughter at a shopping mall. One player is assigned the objective to accidentally leave something behind when she exits the scene. They begin the scene. The character with the objective must find a reason to leave and accidentally forget an object in the playing area.

STATUS EXERCISES

Everyone, in life as well as in theatre, has a certain status. In life, this could be the result of position, wealth and other sources of power. In any grouping, some people will be more popular or more powerful than others. In a theatrical context, the struggle for status is often the basis for a relationship. In any scripted work there will always be a balance of high status characters, low status characters and those who want more status. Understanding a character's status will explain a lot about the choices they make and the way they live out their lives. The following exercises will explore the idea of status and offer ways of playing characters based on their status. Once the concept is understood, it becomes one more way in which a character can be analyzed.

THE PARTY

This exercise is an introduction to the concept of status. The easiest way to understand it is to go with the stereotype that says high status people are generally outgoing and low status people are usually not—extroverts and introverts.

Method: Students form pairs, with the partners on opposite sides of the room. The leader explains that this is a party. The students on the right side of the room are very shy and introverted, and have little self-confidence. They are afraid to meet people at this party. Fortunately, each of them has a friend here who can help them. The students on the left are extroverted, outgoing and confident. It's up to them to go and get their introverted friends, introduce them all around and make sure that they have a good time. The exercise is repeated with the roles reversed.

THE EMPIRE—see CONCENTRATION EXERCISES

This is also a good supplementary exercise to experience status and the lack thereof.

ONE UP

The exercise continues the exploration of status.

Method: In pairs, students simply take turns trying to outdo each other. They carry on a conversation in which everything they say makes them out to be more adventurous, smarter, richer, greater in every way than their partners.

Sample conversation:

A: I had the most fabulous day yesterday. I had a ride in my friend's Porsche.

B: Really? That's nice. I wonder if it can go as fast as my new Ferrari.

A: You own a Ferrari? Well, I don't know if it could beat my friend's Porsche. I'll have to mention it to him while I fly him to Paris in my Lear jet.

Or—a conversation could take the following path:

A: I just got a B+ on that incredibly hard math test.

B: Oh, good for you. Of course, my average in that course in an A.

A: That's nice. Of course, math isn't really my thing. I have an A+ average in English.

B: Oh. Will that get you any scholarships for next year? I'll be on full scholarship to the Harvard School of Business.

The conversations can get as ridiculous as possible and simply end at the command of the leader. No one is going to actually be able to win this one.

Variation #1. As a means of demonstrating that status can come from pathos and sympathy as well as from brains and power, the exercise can be repeated with each partner trying to get below the status of his partner with an even worse hard luck story. The result may look, at first glance, as if the student's status is diminished with every statement, but in fact, while a hard luck story may not give anyone power or influence, the sympathy and attention it can garner is a form of status in itself.

GET HIGHER

Also an exercise to demonstrate the concept of status, in this case by finding a purely physical way to show status.

Method: Pairs work with each other non-verbally. They size each other up and try to take status from the other person. It will begin with a student pulling himself up to his full height, throwing back his shoulders, attempting to look down on his partner, and it may escalate to finding chairs and boxes to stand on in an effort to gain a physical advantage over his partner.

Variation #1. Repeat the exercise with the reverse objective. Students attempt physically to give status to their partners, making themselves lower, physically and figuratively.

PHYSICALIZING STATUS

A discussion about physicalizing status could follow. What are the physical characteristics of a high status character and a low status character?

High Status:

1. Good posture.

2. Makes eye contact easily.

3. Smiling and outgoing, extroverted (or frowning and intimidating).

4. Open body postures—strong and confident.

5. Firm handshake, confident stride of a walk.

Low Status:

1. Slouched posture.

2. Doesn't make eye contact.

3. Shy and introverted.

4. Closed, protective body postures.

6. Afraid of contact, small steps, and tense body movements

This discussion could follow with one on how to take status and how to give it to another character.

Take Status:

1. Order people to do things for you.

2. Put other people down, treat them in a condescending manner—or treat them well and gain status by popularity instead of intimidation.

3. Use big words, name-drop, boast about past deeds.

4. Pause a lot in speech to make people wait for your next words.

5. Follow all physical patterns of a high status character.

Give Status:

1. Ask for advice.

2. Give compliments.

3. Offer to do things for others.

4. Give up physical comfort for others; e.g., offer your chair.

5. Get physically lower than others.

6. Put yourself down.

7. Follow all physical patterns of a low status character.

STATUS IMPROVS

Warm up for status improvs with an audience by having students partner up for some SITUATIONAL IMPROVS (see PARTNER WARM-UPS) with the focus being status. Students a re given characters that are either high or low status and a situation in which to play a scene. Everyone works simultaneously.

Sample Scenes:

1. Co-workers at a fast food restaurant. "A" is high status—been on the job for two months. "B" is low status—first day on the job.

2. Bank Robbers planning their next job. "A" is high status—pulled lots of jobs before, "B" is low status—messed up the last job.

3. Friends at a beach. "A" is high status—lots of friends. "B" is low status—new kid in town.

RANKING

In this improv for an audience, status is completely arbitrary and quite a lot of fun to play with. Students are encouraged to find ways to give people status: treating them kindly, offering compliments and asking for advice. They can take status away by giving those beneath them orders, ignoring them and generally treating them badly. This is best played with all three students being of the same gender, so that it can't become a two against one situation. This exercise is NOT for beginners. Students need experience with less threatening improvisational exercises first.

Premise: This exercise is played with three people. They enter the playing area and silently decide on a ranking for everyone, including themselves. They do not share this information with the audience or with each other. Person number one is the most important person in the scene, number two is below him and number three is at the bottom. They place themselves as one, two or three. They are given a location and begin the scene, treating their number one the best and their number three the worst. After the scene ends, the audience should be able to guess who the actors ranked as numbers one, two and three.

Variation #1. To make it more challenging, it can be played with four people. It could now be played by two students of each gender. Students generally need a little experience at improv before they are successful playing in groups of four, as it is harder for them to listen to each other.

FIND A FRIEND

Perhaps the ultimate struggle for status, in this exercise students come to realize that achieving high status is often more effectively done through kindness leading to popularity, rather than through the power of intimidation. This exercise can be hard on the ego and should not be played early in a session. Students need a little experience with improvisation before they learn to not take it personally. Insure that the scene is played with a gender balance, never only one male with four females, or one female with four males—it is too difficult to avoid "ganging up" on the lone member of the opposite gender.

Premise: This exercise is played with groups of four or five students, who are given a location. Their only objective is to stay in the scene and have one of the other players leave. It becomes an exercise in survival. The only way to insure that you will not be made to leave the scene is to find a friend who wants you to stay. The scene is over when it is clear to the audience that one of the players should leave, whether he has physically done that, or is still fighting an already lost battle.

PULLING FACES

In this exercise, one player is given status by virtue of her position, but the lower-status player can pull rank on her. This is where players find out that playing a low status character can be much more fun than playing one with a lot.

Premise: The scene contains characters with a boss/underling relationship. The boss has all the status. However, it is the objective of the underling to pull silly faces/imitations of the boss whenever possible in the scene, without getting caught by the boss. The scene can be played for a specific length of time, perhaps two minutes, with the audience counting how many faces were pulled successfully. The next underling to play the scene tries to beat the previous score.

SWITCH STATUS

This exercise points out that status is not only a result of one's position in life, it is also a choice to give or take status from another person. Status can be largely a result of a person's confidence level and the way in which they interact with others.

Premise: The scene contains two characters, one in a high status position, the other low. Example: boss/employee or beggar/shopkeeper. They start the scene playing their status; however, at any time the leader can call "Switch" and the status is reversed, although the roles stay the same. Suddenly, the shopkeeper finds ways of giving the beggar status, who finds ways to take it. That is, until the leader calls for another switch.

CREATING A CHARACTER

Many of the exercises in the warm-up activities and all of the exercises in the improvisation chapter, challenge students to work in a character that may or may not be very much like themselves. However, the following exercises focus on the "how to" of creating a character. They will be followed with ideas for turning the exercises into projects and written assignments. The first few exercises will utilize stereotypes; however, they will gradually become more challenging, encouraging the students to look at many aspects of a character's personality.

CHARACTER WALKS

Method: Students are instructed to move around the playing area in "neutral," a natural, nondescript walk. Then the leader calls out a specific character and the students try to interpret this character through the walk.

Sample characters: A monster, an alien, a priest/nun, a robot, a clown, a ghost, a wild animal, a domestic animal, a bird, a Sumo wrestler, a contortionist.

PANTOMIME IN CHARACTER

Method: Students respond to the leader calling out different characters while they are performing a mimed activity. All students are working simultaneously, either on their own, in pairs, or in small groups.

Sample mimed activities:	Sample characters:
Drinking a glass of milk	As an elderly person
	As a truck driver
	As a two-year-old child
Digging a hole	As a gymnast
	As a dentist
	As a lumberjack
Writing a difficult letter	As a prison inmate
	As a bank president
	As a junior high student

Brushing and flossing teeth	As a very ill person
	As a professional wrestler
	As a successful politician

WAITING FOR A BUS

Method: Students take turns performing a pantomime of a character waiting at a bus stop. They choose a character by occupation, finding ways to show this character's occupation by the way they walk, sit and carry themselves. Remind them that they are not at work performing their occupational tasks, they are merely waiting for a bus. The leader can narrate the arrival of the bus in order to end the exercise.

DOMINANT BODY PART

Method:

Step 1. As the students walk around the space in "neutral," the leader calls out a specific body part and encourages students to focus on it, allowing it to change and control the way in which they walk. They actually "lead" with that part of their body to discover how that feels. Example: Nose. How would a walk change if the nose were controlling it? Would the head be held higher as a result?

Step 2. This exercise can lead to characterizations, by having students imagine there is something specific or special about the dominant body part. Example: Nose; it is too big, too small, running because of allergies, perfect—after having a nose job, etc. Students are encouraged to keep walking and explore what kind of a character would be in possession of such a nose. Would this person be an introvert or an extrovert (or in theatre terminology, low status or high)? What sort of job or profession would this person have? Where would he live? Would he have friends?

Step 3. After exploring this exercise with various body parts, ask students to pick their favourite characters from the ones they have created. Have each find her own space in the room and create a world for this character. The leader narrates them through the day of this character, beginning with getting up in the morning, fixing breakfast (or grabbing a coffee on the run), going to work and so on. Narrate them through a good day and then a bad day in the life of this character. As the leader narrates, the students pantomime their characters' actions.

Step 4. Once they have established the daily patterns of this character, have them repeat the day's activities, but allow other characters in the room to interact with theirs.

Step 5. In partner improvisations, place any two characters in a location and have them interact with each other. They retain the characters they have created, but now use them in various environments.

CHARACTER RECALL

This exercise focuses on the student's pantomime skills, but also requires them to create a character by observation.

Students are asked to follow a person in a public place for twenty minutes. They should be very discreet. The idea isn't to get arrested for stalking. They make careful mental note not only of what the person is doing, but also of how they are doing it.

The next class students are given two minutes to perform a pantomime of the person they followed. The audience should know where they are, what they are doing and also have some sense of the age, mental state and personality of the character.

Follow-up assignment #1. Students write a character sketch in which this character is given a complete background, guessing the person's age, occupation, whether they live alone or have a family and anything else they can infer from what they witnessed.

Follow-up assignment #2. Students write a monologue in the voice of their character. This is not simply a reading of the character sketch, but rather students should pretend that their character is speaking specifically to another person. They explore what their character would have to say to someone else in a particular situation. This can be a written assignment as well as a performance for the class.

Variation #1. Instead of following a stranger, students could recall the actions and characteristics of a person they know well. A pantomime, character sketch and monologue could follow.

stages • CREATIVE IDEAS FOR TEACHING DRAMA

LIKE AN ANIMAL

Students will create characters based on animal traits.

Method:

Step 1. Students are asked to move about the space as a jungle animal. They can choose which jungle animal they would like to be, making the sounds and actions of that animal.

Step 2. Students stand and walk upright, but maintain the characteristics of this animal.

Step 3. Students begin to speak English and interact with each other, but retain a trace of this animal in their speech and, more importantly, in their physical characteristics and attitudes. They are human characters, based on their animal's qualities.

Step 4. Students drop their characters and have a discussion about how we view animals. People have personified animals, giving them human characteristics based on what they look like or what they do. This has led to cliché similes: sly like a fox, wise as an owl, hungry as a bear, etc. In this exercise, rather than apply human characteristics to an animal, students use an animal as the base for a human character.

Step 5. Repeat the exercise with everyone becoming a barnyard or domestic animal and then taking those characteristics into a human character.

Step 6. Students choose their favourite character to take to this stage, where they create a physical environment for their character. They may leave their environments to visit other characters in theirs. Remind them that they are playing human characters, not animals. They must find a way to bring the characteristics of their animal into this person.

Examples: A hibernating bear might become an author who likes to write in his den, with a warm fireplace and comfortable chair. He may become quite irritable if anyone disturbs him. Once his book is finished, he wants to go out for a huge meal, with salmon being his favourite food. His voice is gruff and he isn't fond of company.

A pink flamingo might become an interior decorator who is very flamboyant and loves to use colour. She is very gregarious and loves to go to parties, interacting with everyone there. She loves to laugh and makes people feel at ease in her company. She is always well-dressed and groomed, following the latest fashions and very confident. She is also extremely graceful.

Step 7. Students are placed in pairs to improvise a scene involving both of their characters. They repeat the improv, editing until they are happy with the results. The scene should have a beginning, middle and an end. There should be a conflict to be solved. Each character needs an objective, something that they want from the other. The finished scene can be scripted by the partners and rehearsed.

Step 8. Pairs take turns performing their scenes for the whole group. A discussion could follow related to how the actors used and remained true to their animals while interacting in the scene.

LABAN EFFORT ACTIONS

Rudolf Laban was an American modern dancer during the early days of modern dance in the mid-twentieth century. He developed a method of categorizing the way in which the human body can move. He looked at the speed at which a person moved—quickly, or slow and sustained—and called it time. He studied whether a person was direct in getting to where they were going, or indirect, taking the scenic routes of life, and called it space. Lastly, he observed whether a person performed movements that were very ponderous, strong and heavy, or light and airy, and called it weight. He further discovered that if opposites in these three categories were configured, there were eight possible combinations. He called them Effort Actions. Every human on earth could be put into one of those eight categories, as could every character ever written. Each category has a descriptive name. The Effort Actions can be used to define a character in a script, or used as the bases from which a character is created.

Not only can these Effort Actions define a person's physical movement style, they can also define personality traits, the way in which a person functions mentally.

EIGHT EFFORT ACTIONS

NAME		TIME	SPACE	WEIGHT
Press	=	Sustained	Direct	Heavy
Punch	=	Quick	Direct	Heavy
Float	=	Sustained	Indirect	Light
Glide	=	Sustained	Direct	Light
Wring	=	Sustained	Indirect	Heavy
Slash	=	Quick	Indirect	Heavy
Flick	=	Quick	Indirect	Light
Dab	=	Quick	Direct	Light

In order to assist students in understanding these Effort Actions and developing ways to use them, the following exercise is helpful.

FINDING THE EFFORT ACTIONS

Method: Spread students out in the playing area. Ask them to focus on a spot at the other side of the room and to go straight there. Once they are there, direct them to go back to their original spot, still in a straight line, but with slow, heavy elephant steps. Then explain to the group that what they have done is a personality called a "Press," someone who is very direct, doesn't give up easily, but just plods along towards his goal, no matter who or what might stand in his way. Go through each subsequent Effort Action, naming the Action after they discovered its physicality. Finally, explain that these are called Effort Actions, developed by a modern dancer, Rudolf Laban, in the 1940s.

USING THE EFFORT ACTIONS

Method: Using first the Improv in Pairs technique of having all students work simultaneously and then moving to Improvs with an Audience, assign or have students select a specific Effort Action to use as the basis for a character in an improvised situation. The situation can be replayed by having students switch to a different Effort Action, resulting in quite a different scene.

Variation #1. In addition to using Effort Actions in improvised scenes, students can use them alone, or in conjunction with other methods of creating a character, to write monologues or two-handers (a scene with two characters).

COLOUR CHARACTERIZATION

Another way of looking at someone's character is to describe him or her in terms of a colour. This is a way of saying what kind of personality a colour would have if it were a person, a simple personification of colour.

YELLOW — Bright, sunny, cheerful, extroverted, caring, speaks before thinking.

ORANGE — Extroverted, popular, irresponsible, forgetful, disorganized, doesn't follow through with plans, insensitive, lives for the moment.

RED — Extroverted, intense, plays emotions to the limit, extreme behaviour.

PINK — Very spiritual, kind, in their own world, spaced out, introverted or extroverted.

PURPLE — Very intelligent, witty, snobby, bossy, may be hurtful and cruel, extroverted.

MAUVE — Combination of purple and pink, intelligent and spiritual, witty but kind, introverted.

GREEN — Earthy, natural, not afraid of change, brave, helpful, extrovert.

BLUE — Very organized, punctual, leader, serious, sensitive, afraid of change, hides emotions, introverted.

GRAY — Will take on other people's personalities, like a spy who wants to blend in.

BROWN — More extreme than gray, will actually imitate others.

BLACK — Evil or mysterious, powerful.

WHITE — Very innocent, pure, usually only young children are pure white.

A character may be a combination of colours, or have a dominant colour and another that is secondary.

In the same way it's said that opposites attract, characters opposite to each other on the colour wheel will play off of each other well in a scene. Example: Red/Green, Yellow/Purple, Blue/Orange, Black/White.

PERSONALITY TESTS

Yet one more way of defining a character is through a personality test. There are dozens of systems, but most draw from the same source, Hippocrates. In ancient Greece he laid out a series of personality traits that, grouped together, could tell people which of the humours of the blood ruled their lives. There were four of them: Sanguine, Choleric, Melancholy and Phlegmatic, each with positive and negative affects on the personality.

HIPPOCRATES' HUMOURS OF THE BLOOD

Sanguine	Talkative, expressive, impulsive, emotional, likes to be the centre of attention, charming, enthusiastic, forgetful.
Choleric	Domineering, impatient, strong-willed, born leader, dynamic, organized, confident, goal-oriented.
Melancholic	Analytical, artistic, thoughtful, perfectionist, moody, hard to please, suspicious, prone to depression.
Phlegmatic	Easy-going, quiet, dry wit, sympathetic, unmotivated, selfish, shy, fearful, worried, avoids responsibility.

A character might be a combination of humours.

An easy way to understand these character types is to imagine each of them involved in a group project. The Sanguine would volunteer to present the material once the project was completed. The Choleric would keep everyone organized and on task. The Melancholic would do the research and the art work. The Phlegmatic would offer moral support while doing as little of the work as possible.

AN INTERVIEW

Another way of spontaneously creating a character that can then be fleshed out with analysis under the preceding categories is to conduct an interview with each student.

Method: One at a time, students are asked to sit on a chair in the middle of the space while the leader simply interviews them, asking for their names and ages, occupations, hopes and dreams. They are instructed to be anyone they would like to be, except themselves. They can be asked what they remember to be the best day of their lives, or the worst, about their relationships to other significant people in their lives, but not what colour, humour, animal or Effort Action they resemble. After the interview, they write out a character sketch in which they analyze the character they have become and make decisions about which categories they fit into.

CHARACTER SKETCH

Given all of the preceding ways of approaching characterization, a character could be created for future use in a monologue or scene. A fully developed character sketch would include the following information:

1. What is this character's background information: age, family makeup, physical description, occupation, hopes, dreams and desires?

2. If the character were an animal, what kind of animal would he be and why?

3. What is his dominant body part and why?

4. Which Effort Action is he? Give an example from his life that demonstrates it.

5. Describe this character as a colour.

6. Which of Hippocrates' humours does he most resemble and why?

7. Is this a low or high status character? Is he comfortable with his status?

If writing this character sketch about a character from a play or from real life, the following questions would also help to understand who he really is:

1. What does he say about himself?

2. What do others say about him?

3. What does he do (for actions speak louder than words)?

WRITING A MONOLOGUE

There are many books of monologues for young actors that can be used for workshop performance and character analysis, as well as providing examples of how a monologue is constructed. If students are writing their own monologues, they could consider the following points.

- A well written monologue is character driven. It is written from this character's point of view, not merely a story about an event.

- It is generally best, and easiest, to pretend that the character is speaking to another person. They can imagine the reaction of the other character to things that they say and allow these reactions to push the dialogue further. This doesn't mean that they pause for the other character's response, but rather, that they imagine the other character giving them a look that they interrupt as positive or negative.

- The monologue should talk about something that allows for a range of emotions, or at least one shift in emotion, as one of the purposes of performing a monologue (especially in an audition setting) is to showcase the actor's ability. Therefore, the traits of the character that are being demonstrated are at least as important as the actual spoken material.

- A monologue is not a simple reworking of a character sketch, but shows what the character is like. Rather than describing himself to the audience, a character uses what he finds interesting to talk about and the way in which he talks, to show the audience who he is.

- While the issue of status is present for every character, it may be more useful in a monologue to decide whether the character will project an air of vulnerability or strength. If two contrasting monologues are being sought or written, this issue would be as important a consideration for contrast as whether the two pieces were classical and modern.

- Generally, a suitable length for a monologue is five hundred words.

WRITING A SCENE

There may be a time when it is interesting for students to take an improvised scene and script it. This is an easier approach to scene writing than to simply sit down and decide to write a scene from scratch. The following points should be considered when editing an improvised scene, or when writing a new scene.

- The scene should have a beginning, a middle and an end. This doesn't mean that everything is resolved at the end, as this is not necessarily a whole play, but only that there has been some plot progression moving it forward.

- Each character must have an objective, something that they want from the other character, a reason for remaining in the scene. Objectives should be phrased as a positive, rather than an negative. "I want...," rather than, "I don't want..." These objectives should be fairly concrete, phrased as an action rather than an emotion. "I want...," rather than, "I feel...."

- There should be obstacles put in the path of the characters, making it difficult to get what they want.

- Conflict is much more interesting to play and to watch than harmony. The objective of one character should not mesh easily with that of the other character's.

- Consideration should be given to status. Are these characters of equal or different status? Are they both comfortable with the status they have in relation to the other character or is the struggle for status part of the conflict?

performance
EXERCISES

GROUP PERFORMANCE EXERCISES

These exercises are planned in small groups for a short amount of time (five to ten minutes), with the resulting scene being shared with the rest of the group. The first exercises can be played early in the session, as they have easy problems to solve. They become increasingly complex, containing more difficult problems to solve.

SPECTATOR SPORTS

Problem: The group must decide on a sport that they are all watching together. The way in which they are reacting to the game should tell the audience which sport they are watching.

MOVING DAY

Problem: The group must decide on an object that they are all moving together. The way in which they handle the imaginary object should tell the audience what it is.

MOVED BY AN OBJECT

Problem: The group must decide on an object or force that is moving all of them. The way in which they mime their coordinated movements should tell the audience what is moving them.

MACHINES

Problem: The group must invent a machine. The machine must have a purpose. Every group member must have a sound and repetitive movement that becomes part of the machine. This exercise could follow an introduction to the concept of tableaux.

Variation #1. Instead of the machine having a purpose, it could be an abstract machine that simply has a theme.

Sample themes: Sports fan Machine   Love Machine
                          Peace Machine   Music Machine
                          Eating Machine   Fear Machine

ENTANGLEMENTS

Problem: The group decides on, or is given, an object or environment in which they are literally entangled. They perform a pantomime in which they try to help each other break free.

Sample entanglements:

> Snow—after an avalanche
> A tube of super-glue opened and shared
> Encountering a man-eating plant in the jungle
> Underwater octopus attack
> Walking into quicksand
> Accidentally entering a snake den
> Sand—after a desert windstorm

EMOTION ORCHESTRA

Problem: The group chooses a conductor. Each member of her orchestra chooses an emotion. They perform the emotion's symphonic piece for the whole group, in which the conductor cues in specific emotions, indicating their volume and duration, blending them together to create a piece. Orchestra members find sounds to vocalize representing their specific emotions, but they do not speak actual words.

SLOW MOTION

Problem: Group members choose a sport to play in extreme slow motion. It may be done with a narrator off to the side providing the colour commentary.

THE BODY

Problem: "You are minding your own business when you stumble upon a body." What happens next? The group must plan a scene showing the finding of a body and what follows. It could be done in pantomime, or with dialogue.

THE ACCIDENT

Problem: "There's been an accident." What happens next? The group must plan a scene involving an accident and how it is dealt with. It could be done in pantomime or with dialogue.

RESCUE TEAM

Problem: The group decides on, or is given, a catastrophic event that has caused them to form a rescue team. Together they pantomime their feat of daring, rescuing imaginary people or animals.

Sample rescue efforts: Battle a blaze in a forest
Try to enter a burning house
Climb a tree to rescue a cat
Save people on rooftops during a flood
Dig out miners after a cave-in

Variation #1. Instead of forming a rescue team, the group is in need of rescue and pantomimes their collective escape effort after a catastrophic event.

CRIME OF THE CENTURY

Problem: The group decides on the perfect crime and re-enacts it in pantomime, or in a scene with dialogue.

COLLECTION OF OBJECTS

Problem: The group portrays a collection of objects that would be found together. A group could pick their collection from a deck of cards held by the leader, or could come up with their own. Each group member becomes one of the objects in the collection. It could be performed in pantomime, or with dialogue. If dialogue is used, students speak to each other in their roles as the objects, but cannot actually name any of the objects or what type of collection they are. This should be made clear to the audience by the skill of the pantomime and the subtle hints in the dialogue.

Sample collections:

> Cans of food on a store shelf
> Makeup on a bathroom counter top
> Pop bottles in a machine
> Fillings in a sandwich
> Medicines in a medicine cabinet
> Clothes in a washer or dryer
> Books in a bookstore
> Cutlery in a drawer
> Food in a refrigerator
> School supplies in a locker
> Objects in a woman's purse

SPORTS

Problem: Groups prepare a scene with a sports theme. The theme could be picked from a deck of cards or be decided on by the group. The scene should have a beginning, middle and an end. It should contain a conflict and a resolution. It is not merely playing the chosen sport.

Sample sports environments:

Curling rink	Baseball dugout
Hockey arena	Swimming pool
Figure skating rink	Wrestling ring
Bowling alley	Ski jump
Diving pool	Car racing pit
Tennis court	Basketball court

CHARACTER ON THE OUTSIDE

Problem: Groups plan a scene in which all but one person in the group play characters that are alike. The other person plays a complementary character. Each scene contains a conflict between the main set of characters and the other. Groups can pick from a deck of cards or choose their own character group.

Sample character groups:

> Co-workers and a boss
> Team members and a coach
> Students and a teacher
> Teachers and a principal
> Medical team and a patient
> Restaurant patrons and a waiter
> Pets and an owner

WAITING

Problem: The group decides on a group of characters who are together in a location waiting for something. All characters are waiting for the same thing. The leader could give the groups that something.

For example:

- Everyone is waiting for a bell to ring. The groups decide who they are and why they are waiting for the bell. They could be school children outside (or inside) waiting for the recess bell, mental hospital patients waiting for activity time, seniors waiting for the dinner bell, etc.

- Everyone is waiting for a person. The groups could be pets and owners waiting for the vet, people in a courtroom waiting for the jury to return, children waiting for a parent to tuck them in at night, etc.

- Everyone is waiting to do something: The groups could be passengers waiting to board a plane, people at a bus stop, people trapped in a cave waiting for rescue, etc.

NOTE: In beginning classes, the scene could be very short and done only in pantomime. The audience tries to get a sense of the location and characters from the way the pantomime is carried out. For more advanced students, dialogue could be added.

TRANSFORM AN OBJECT

Problem: Each group is given a simple household object, picked at random from a bag. This object must be incorporated into a scene. Every group member must use it at some point in the scene. Each time it is used, it transforms into something else.

Variation #1. The object could be so large that instead of a hand prop it becomes a set piece, transforming as the need arises.

Examples: Chair, ladder, mime box, platform, table, bench, large cardboard box, etc.

PROPS

Problem: Each group is given a bag containing a collection of hand props, simple everyday objects. They plan a scene, making each object an important part of the story.

HATS

Problem: Each group is given a bag of hats, enough for everybody to wear one. Each person works out a character based on his or her hat. The characters work out a scene in which they all play a part.

Variation #1. As in the exercise to transform an object, each group receives only one hat. Group members take turns wearing it, becoming a different character each time they receive the hat.

NOUNS AND VERBS

Problem: Each group picks a noun from one deck of cards and a verb from another deck. They must create a scene, keeping the noun and the verb central to the plot line. The leader may prepare the cards before the lesson, or each person writes out one noun and one verb on separate cards, which are then collected for use.

VERBS ONLY

Problem: Each group must decide on an activity they are doing together, or it can be picked from a deck of cards with suggestions. No preparation time is given to plan the scene. It is improvised, using one word at a time instead of whole sentence dialogue. The words used must be verbs.

Sample activities: Building a house, flying a kite, catching a tiger, training a dog, hunting a bear, etc.

FOREIGNERS

Problem: Group decides on, or is given, a location and an activity. No preparation time is given, except to decide on which country each character comes from. The scene is improvised with the characters trying to keep their own accents clear and not copying another's.

Sample locations and activities: Judges at an Olympic event. A train derails in Europe. Business partners discuss an international merger. A group of passengers wait to board a late flight, etc.

COMIC REPETITION OF THREE

Problem: Each group prepares a scene in which an event happens repetitively. Everything is predictable on the first two repetitions. On the third repetition, something surprising happens. It may be helpful to give them one scenario to play, as a practice, before they develop their own; e.g., pop machine that works fine (or not) twice, with something different happening when the third person tries to buy a pop.

CIRCLE STORY SCENES—see GROUP WARM-UPS, CIRCLE STORY, Variation #4

The small group makes a circle story, then re-enacts it for the whole group, with one person narrating it and the rest performing it in pantomime.

Variation #1. The story is told one sentence at a time. When the group mimes the story, each person narrates his or her own sentence.

Variation #2. In a small group, players share their worst nightmares. Then they chose their favourite to re-enact for the whole group. The player who owns the nightmare is involved in the pantomime, narrating it in the first person singular.

Variation #3. Instead of a worst nightmare, players share the worst (or best) day of their lives and choose one person to re-enact it.

Variation #4. Instead of narrated pantomime, the story is enacted with dialogue.

TIME AND PLACE

Problem: Each group picks an environment suggestion from a deck of cards, or creates their own; e.g., an Old West saloon, a space station in the year 2525, a science lab, a Neanderthal cave, the Yukon gold rush, a medieval castle, a 1940s movie set. The group then decides on the characters in this environment and create a scene for them to interact with each other. Or, they can stop the preparation once they have found their own characters, and improvise the scene.

THE MEAL

Problem: Groups must decide on a location in which everyone in the group will eat a meal. They also pick a topic of conversation not related to the meal or the location. The mime for the food and the location must be made clear without ever being mentioned in the conversation.

Sample locations and conversations:

> Friends eat together in a fast food joint and talk about their plans for the weekend.

> A young family has Sunday dinner at Grandma's house and talks about their last vacation.

COMMON LOCATION

Problem: Groups are given a common location. Every student in the group must find his own character and reason for being in this location (the character's objective). Once chosen, groups improvise the scene, having their characters interact with each other. Each character must focus on playing his own objective, using the other characters to achieve it.

Sample locations and reasons:

Movie Theatre	Characters
	An elderly person looking for company
	A young person trying to pick up a date
	A thief hiding out after robbing a store
	A singer who considers herself to be famous
	Someone who just wants to watch the movie

Bus Depot	A grandmother going to visit the kids
	A nervous kid off to college for the first time
	An illegal immigrant going to hide out
	A farm kid off to the big city to find a job
	A pet owner going to a big show
	A rock star wannabe off to a talent contest

HISTORICAL FIGURE

Problem: The group plans a scene in which a well-known historical figure finds him or herself in another era, a different time in history.

Sample figures and eras:

Christopher Columbus in a supermarket
Queen Victoria in a Neanderthal cave
Einstein in an Old West fort
Galileo in a modern science museum

SILENT TREATMENT

Problem: Group plans a scene in which all but one character are in the same location and have a good reason to be furious with each other. They want to speak to each other, but cannot. Finally, the remaining character enters, breaks the silence and finds an ending to the scene.

SCENE WITH CONDITIONS

Problem: Groups must create a scene containing a set of three random conditions, which were picked from a deck of cards in the leader's hand.

Sample conditions:

There is a character that only speaks at the end
One character walks with a cane—for a reason
There is a couple in love
One character gets injured
There is a surprise in the middle of the scene
Something sad happens
A character brings bad news

A character wins something
One character is a small child
The weather turns bad
The scene contains a natural disaster
The scene contains a wedding
One character can't speak English
Two characters are twins—one evil, one good
Something breaks during the scene

REAL LIFE SITUATION

Problem: The group—of no more than three or four students—must plan a scenario containing a problem or issue that's easy for them to relate to in their own age and stage of life. The issue is serious and the scene is played for realism, not for the audience's entertainment. No preparation time is allowed to rehearse the scene. Once a scenario has been decided upon, groups take turns performing their improvisations. This exercise may not be suitable for very young children.

Sample issues:

Older children
> One child must tell the others that he is moving away.
> One child tells the others he just found out his parents are getting a divorce.
> The group tells a child they are sorry his pet died.

Teenagers
> A girl tells her friends she is pregnant.
> A teen shows her parents her new tattoo.
> A teen wants to get a motorcycle.
> A teen wants to leave home before graduation.

Adults
> Parents and teacher discuss a child.
> Co-workers discuss leaving a job.
> Siblings discuss caring for an aged parent.

ECCENTRICS

Problem: Group is given an eccentric behaviour that must be demonstrated by one or two of their members in an otherwise normal setting.

Sample eccentricities:

Someone:

> thinks she sees a ghost:
> forgets everything she is told
> thinks she is a famous person
> finds everything extremely funny
> is very paranoid
> thinks she is an alien from space
> can channel for a long dead person
> can predict the future
> thinks everyone is a long lost relative
> has forgotten her name
> hates to be touched—at all

NARRATION/DIALOGUE

Problem: Group decides on a location and a reason for characters to be there. One member narrates the story for the audience, one sentence at a time. The rest of the group pantomimes the action, taking turns to provide one line of dialogue for each line of narration. The dialogue directly relates to the narration.

Example: "The day was a hot one." "Wow, what a scorcher."

BLEND THE SCENES

Problem: Groups plan a simple scene with characters interacting in a non-specific environment. Then two groups perform their scenes simultaneously, listening and incorporating the other group's scene into their own, blending the two together.

LECTURE—see TABLEAUX EXERCISES

INDIVIDUAL PERFORMANCE EXERCISES

WHERE HAVE YOU BEEN?

Method: Students take turns performing for each other. They open the door to the space one by one, with a short pantomime that shows where they have been.

Example: A student enters and mimes shaking out a wet umbrella, indicating that she has just come inside out of the rain. Students are encouraged to trust their imaginations and not worry about planning their entrances. By the time they turn the doorknob to open the door, an idea will come to them. (See third rule of improv—Go with your first idea, it's probably your best one.)

TAKE THE STAGE

Method: One at a time, students go to the front of the group, which applauds wildly for them. The student silences the crowd, performs the first thing that he thinks of, bows, accepts the applause and leaves the stage area. The audience goes wild for the next performer. The "act" itself can be anything at all. It need take only a few seconds to perform.

IMITATE AND EXAGERATE

This exercise introduces students to the basis for physical comedy, which is imitation and exaggeration.

Method: One at a time, students take the stage, where a chair has been placed. The first student sits on the chair, says hello to the audience and leaves. Each subsequent student imitates the actions of the preceding student, exaggerating everything she did. When it has gone as far as it can go, the next student starts with a new "act." This exercise can, of course, be repeated without a chair, or with some other set piece.

STORY IN A MINUTE

This exercise helps students to organize their thoughts and use their imaginations to create a scenario. It also allows them to develop a performance piece in a non-threatening way, as all students work simultaneously in the first stages. When they reach the final performance stage, they should be familiar with the material and comfortable about using it.

Method: Students are given the first line of self-narration. They say it aloud and continue speaking for one minute, filling in details and acting out their stories as they create them. Halfway through the minute, they must bring a change of emotion into their stories.

Example first line:

> "But something had changed since I was here last."
> "It felt so strange to the touch."
> "I knew that if it didn't stop I would scream."

The entire project runs as follows:

1. Students narrate their own stories simultaneously for one minute. They stay on their feet, to allow for action.
2. The exercise is repeated, giving students an opportunity to edit and refine their story ideas. Again, it is timed to be exactly one minute. The leader calls out the thirty-second and forty-five second points to assist students in planning the timing of events in their stories.
3. Students take turns telling their stories to a partner, who acts out the story spontaneously. This allows them to view their own stories and to decide if there is enough action in the plot line, whether it has a satisfying ending, and to determine if there is any more editing they would like to do.
4. Final rehearsal. Again, everyone is working simultaneously, narrating and pantomiming their story. The story is timed.
5. Each student narrates and performs the action of their story for the whole group.

WAITING FOR A BUS—see CREATING A CHARACTER EXERCISES

CHARACTER RECALL—see CREATING A CHARACTER EXERCISES

MONOLOGUES—see CREATING A CHARACTER EXERCISES

student group
PROJECTS

STORYTELLING

A group project on storytelling is a good introduction to extended group work as well as to performance. The project would likely take three sessions, from introduction to completed performances. In the first session the genre could be introduced, groups formed, and stories handed out to group members who could take turns reading aloud to their group. The second session would be for rehearsals. The third session would allow each group a fast run-through with performances to follow.

Method:

1. Students are given, or choose stories, several pages in length. Generally the whole group will work within the same genre, with each smaller group presenting stories from that genre. Legends, myths, fairy tales, parables and fables all work well.

2. The group becomes familiar with their story.

3. Two or more narrators are chosen to tell the audience the story IN THEIR OWN WORDS, while the rest of the group pantomimes the story for the audience.

Hints:

1. Pointer sheets may be held by the narrators to help keep them on track.

2. A box of simple costume pieces and appropriate props for the genre might be made available for each group to use in turn.

Evaluation could focus on teamwork during the process and on concentration during the performance, with bonus points for creativity.

MUSIC MIME

This exercise works well after some introductory lessons involving movement, such as FLUID TABLEAUX, pantomime exercises such as HEADLINES, and some warm-up individual music mime exercises, in which a piece of music is played for the group, who sit with their eyes closed and listen. The music is played again and students are encouraged to pantomime a story to go with the music, each in their own playing area. After several pieces of music in various styles, the group will be ready for a group project developing their own music mime.

Method:

1. The group is divided into smaller groups of five or six students each.

2. Each group chooses a piece of instrumental music two to three minutes in length. Or, if space and equipment are a concern, one piece of music is played and all groups work with it.

3. The music is listened to several times, after which the small group brainstorms story ideas to go with the music.

4. Story ideas are improvised and rehearsed until the action fits the mood, tempo and dynamics of the music perfectly.

5. Each small group performs their music mime for the large group.

Variation #1. Costumes, props and set pieces may be added.

Variation #2. As part of a unit on mask work; white face or character masks may be used. The use of masks tends to help the students make their movements more stylized and clearer. Care must be taken to use open body positions in order to share with the audience. The audience needs to see the actor's masked face full frontal at all times in order to relate to the character.

FAIRYTALE THEATRE

This method of enacting a fairytale takes a story from the written page to a piece of theatre in five easy steps. It works best with groups of six to eight members.

Method:

Step 1. The story is read to or by the group.

Step 2. The story is divided into five or six "chapters," with a tableau created that best describes the action of each chapter. This tableau can be thought of as a title page illustration. All actors are involved in each tableau. If there are too many actors, they become inanimate objects needed to complete the picture.

Step 3. Mimed action is added to string all the tableaux together. Actors pause slightly to show each tableau.

Step 4. The mime is repeated without pausing at each tableau. Actors simultaneously narrate the action, as well as the dialogue of their own characters. This is the stage in which all the clever bits are discovered. The group rehearses the piece again, listening to each other and deciding how much narration to keep for the final step.

Step 5. The story is repeated as a performance piece. For the final product, the narration may continue or may be dropped as dialogue between the characters is added. The group might also decide to have only one narrator. In any case, there will be full dialogue between characters.

The steps are easily remembered by the following key words:

1. Read

2. Tableaux

3. Pantomime

4. Self-narration

5. Dialogue

Variation #1. Nursery rhymes may be used for young children or as a warm-up when the project is first introduced. A new tableau is created for each line of the rhyme.

Variation #2. The group may rewrite traditional fairytales. For example:

1. The story is updated and set in modern times (or in the disco 70s, or rock and roll 50s, etc.)

2. The ending of a traditional story may be changed.

3. Some of the characters from two or more stories may be combined to create a new story.

4. The group may write a totally new fairytale.

Variation #3. Many other story sources may be used, such as Native legends, fables or Greek mythology.

ANCIENT RITUALS

Exploring the concept of rituals and ultimately writing and performing their own rituals is a good way to end of unit of voice work. It combines elements of choral speech, repetitive movement and music mime. (See Litany for the Moon— VOICE EXERCISES.)

Method:

1. The group is introduced to the concept of rituals. Modern rituals can be explored, such as weddings, funerals, church services, etc. Research can be done to uncover ancient rituals, such as ceremonies of coronations, burials, sacrifice, worship, rain dances, etc.

2. Improvisations can be performed, first using modern, and then ancient rituals as their bases.

3. Groups of six to eight students are formed.

4. The requirements for the assignment are handed out and discussed.

5. Each group chooses a ritual to enact. This may be based on an actual ancient ritual, or may be invented by the group.

6. Rehearsal time is given.

7. Each group performs their ritual for the group, or a wider audience. For example, in a high school, the ancient rituals could be presented as a noon-hour performance at Halloween. Donations or admittance charges could be accepted and donated to UNICEF.

Sample assignment for Ancient Rituals

Requirements:

1. The ritual must be between five and ten minutes in length.

2. The ritual must have a purpose, with a beginning, middle and end.

3. The characters involved must all have a role, or function in the ritual.

4. The ritual must be set to music (instrumental only).

5. There must be some sections of repetitive movement.

6. There must be some sections with sounds, both vocal and created with objects or instruments (tambourines, drums, sticks, etc.). Actual words, if any, should be kept to a minimum.

Costumes, or at least some simple costume pieces, could be added for public performance.

Evaluation could be based on the originality of the piece, the fulfillment of requirements and the focus of the group in their use of rehearsal time.

READER'S THEATRE

This traditional form of theatre is still widely used as a way of presenting material, both scripted and original. It is great for classrooms and other workshop or performance situations where a lengthy rehearsal process is not desirable. Reader's Theatre acts as a bridge between choral speaking and formal theatre. Oral interpreters vocally bring the material to life, relying on the audience to use their imaginations to fill in the action.

Reader's Theatre has traditionally worked with very specific stage conventions. Once the audience accepted what they saw used on stage during a Reader's Theatre presentation, they were able to accept these conventions without having them interfere with the reality created by the readers.

Conventions of Traditional Reader's Theatre:

- Readers sat on stools. They turned their backs on the audience if they weren't in a particular scene.

- Off-stage focus was used. The readers looked at each other in an imaginary mirror placed in front of the stage, rather than looking directly at each other.

- Scripts were placed in folders, usually on music stands in front of their stools. Although dialogue was almost memorized, the material was read during performance.

- Scripts generally called for a narrator, who spoke directly to the audience.

- Costumes were not used. Readers usually wore neutral clothing, such as all black.

- Readers could play multiple characters.

Now, traditional conventions may still be used, or the presentation can move a little closer to formal theatre. Perhaps actors hold their scripts and some stage movements are used. Actors might use on-stage focus during dialogue and costume pieces could be added. Instead of sitting on stools, mime boxes or ladders could be used as set pieces or for permanent reader placement, if movement was not being used.

The process for developing a piece of Reader's Theatre depends on whether an already scripted piece is being used, or if the group is writing their own script.

Process for a scripted piece:

1. Choose play or story.

2. Cast roles. In the case of a story, the narration may be divided between several readers. Some of the narration may be turned into dialogue, to allow for more changes of voices.

3. Decide on conventions to be used.

4. Rehearse.

5. Present.

Process for a thematic self-created piece:

1. Choose theme.

2. Gather appropriate material related to theme—stories, poems, song lyrics, comics, jokes, quotes, news articles, etc.

3. Review and select material to be included.

4. Find logical order for material.

5. Create bridges and transitions from one item to the next.

6. Read through and edit.

7. Decide on conventions to be used.

8. Rehearse.

9. Present.

Sample Reader's Theatre Assignment: thematic approach

Requirements:

1. Piece should be between four and seven minutes in length.

2. A minimum of five different sources should be used, from a minimum of three difference genres.

   For example: two poems, two jokes, one story; or, 1one song lyric, two quotes, two news articles.

3. All readers should have an equal role to play.

Evaluation could be based on the quality of the material, use of rehearsal time, as well as the final presentation. The presentation grade could be based on the clarity and audibility of the readers, the flow of the material and the characterizations and variety of the voices, as well as fulfilling the source requirements.

COLLAGE COLLECTIVES

Like a thematic Reader's Theater presentation, a Collage Collective is a piece created by a group who has collected material and formed it into a cohesive whole. The difference is that a Collage Collective uses many different forms of theatrical presentation, including, but not limited to, Reader's Theatre.

In a Collage Collective, all material may come from published sources, but frequently, the group will develop some of the material, with improvisation being the primary tool.

Advantages of Collage Collectives over traditional theatre with scripted plays:

1. Everyone in the group can play a role of equal size and importance.

2. The rehearsal process is much shorter.

3. Each group member can contribute creatively to the material, thereby establishing a sense of ownership to the project.

4. It creates an opportunity for individual talents to be utilized, by including songs, dances, mimes and any other talent an actor brings to the group.

5. Students develop a sense of community as they contribute to the project.

Applications of this project:

A Collage Collective can be used by a variety of different groups and for different purposes.

1. As a course assignment, the groups may be made up of five to eight students, with everyone playing an equal role in finding, sorting and creating the material. They would rehearse it independently and present it before the desired audience— either the rest of the class or a larger audience. It becomes a true collaborative effort.

2. As a performance piece for a large group of actors, it is best to have a director. In large groups it is very difficult to have everyone make all decisions collaboratively. It is much more

efficient to have one person with the final say. Also, with a large cast, someone must be able to sit back and see the stage picture and block the action. This is especially important if the final presentation is meant for a paying audience from the general public, in which case even a small group could benefit from working with a director.

The process will be slightly different in each scenario.

Process for a small Group Collective—no leader:

1. Choose theme.

2. Collect suitable material.

3. Brainstorm possible scenarios for improvs related to the theme.

4. Improv scenarios, possibly tape/digitally recording them for future scripting.

5. Choose material, balancing found material with improvised scenes.

6. Choose mode of presentation for each piece—song, dance, Reader's Theatre, mime, instrumental, puppets, circus acts, etc.

8. Decide which actors will take on which roles and present various pieces of the material.

9. Place all material in a logical order.

10. Create transitions from one piece to the next.

11. Run through piece several times, editing along the way.

12. Set stage movements and use of set pieces and props.

13. Rehearse.

14. Present.

Some cautionary notes:

1. Encourage groups to steer away from improvising so much material with the same characters and storyline that they try to turn it into a play. A play takes careful script analysis and character development that is usually well beyond the time allotment for a project of this nature. It is better to have

several small scenes based on the theme interspersed with other source material.

2. Consider the audience for which this piece will be presented. It will have a different tone if it is set for an audience of peers, young children or the general public. The subject matter and language content and level should be appropriate for the target audience.

3. The performance space will determine the amount of movement the piece will contain as well as the technical aspects of the show. Typically, since the piece is a thematic collage rather than a play, lighting, sets, and props can be kept to a bare minimum.

Sample assignment for small group collective:
Requirements:

1. Piece should be between ten and fifteen minutes in length.

2. Material should come from a minimum of six different sources, from a minimum of four different genres. One of these genres must be improvisation. In this way, the material will be a combination of original and found materials.

   For example: one story, one mime set to music, three improvs, one poem, or two jokes, two improvs, one play excerpt, one dance, or one quote, two songs, two improvs, one excerpt of a scripted puppet show.

Evaluation for this group assignment might focus on teamwork throughout the process as well as the final product. A grade could be given for fulfilling the source requirements, creativity and originality, focus and flow of material and overall execution.

Process for large Group Collective—with director or leader:

1. Choose theme.

2. Collect suitable material.

3. Do a variety of exercises to create original material (suggestions to follow).

4. Director oversees writing of the script from material generated by the group.

5. Director casts roles.

6. Run-throughs, with editing as needed.

7. Director sets stage movement and use of set pieces and props.

8. Rehearse.

9. Present.

Exercises to generate material:

1. Very early in the process, the theme may be explored using visual art. A large roll of paper is laid out on the floor, providing each group member with a drawing station of approximately one foot in length, around the paper. Each station has a few colours to work with—crayons, felt markers or pencil crayons. On the command to begin, each member begins to draw a picture of what the theme means to him or her. After one minute, the leader calls for the actors to move, and each person continues the drawing of the actor to her right. This continues until all actors are back at their original stations. A discussion on the results follows, often providing insight into how everyone interprets the theme.

2. A sharing circle may be created, with group members seated on the floor. As a small object is passed around the circle, each person gives a sentence or two on what the theme means to him or her. The object can go around several times. Actors are free to pass or speak. Immediately following the circle, group members independently write a page about what they heard in the circle. They can include what they said and what others said. It can be in point form or in paragraphs. It could be done in the first person singular or third person. It could even be written as dialogue, with "he said," and "she said." The writings are collected to be used in the scripting of the final piece. One sentence could be quoted, or a larger piece could become a monologue. It could be used as a dialogue between two or more actors, or each actor could speak one line at a time individually to create a running narrative, for a time, by the whole group. One word or phrase

could be repeated, or used in canon, to create a soundscape. The possibilities are endless.

3. Group members could be asked to bring in a small object related to the theme and of some significance to them. The object could be the focus of an improvisation, or used symbolically in a more subtle way.

4. Tableaux can be used to great effect in collectives. It may be that a full group tableau could open and/or close the piece. When actors are not involved in a part of the piece, they could move back into their places in the tableau instead of leaving the stage. For example, several ladders, chairs, boxes, raisers or other set pieces could be arranged on the stage, with actors occupying different positions on the set.

Tableaux can also be an interesting way of approaching the improvisations of the piece.

Method: Two or three aspects of the theme are identified. For example, the theme is "The future." Two aspects, or categories, of this theme that will be dealt with are Hopes and Fears. Students are asked to think of a situation that they could find themselves in, in relation to each category. They then take a mental photograph of this situation. They pose in a tableau of themselves in this photo and describe the photo to the group. The director listens and picks one short phrase from this description as the title for the tableau. For example, a student creates a tableau under the category, "Fear." In her tableau, she is doubled over as if in pain. She describes her photo, saying, "I am afraid that I'll develop an incurable disease, like other members of my family. I can't move, can't get past the pain. The idea of suffering pain paralyzes me." The director chooses the phrase, "can't get past the pain," as the title of this tableau. At the end of the exercise, about five students' tableaux are chosen to represent each of the categories. These five tableaux can be treated in any number of ways. For example:

1. The tableaux can be repeated by all five students, creating a movement pattern. This can be featured or

used as background action for a scene, poem,
monologue or song.

2. The owner of each tableaux can repeat the others',
holding their own when the group reaches it.

3. The student can say his tableau title to another
student, using it as the first line of an improv. The
improv ends when the pair reach the second actor's
title, which becomes the first line of an improv
between the second and third actors in the group.
Finally, the last improv is performed between the fifth
actor and the first actor who began the exercise.

4. The titles of the tableaux can be used as a litany or
chant, with or without the tableaux.

5. An actor can pose in her tableau, say its title, and have
it imitated by the other four actors, or by the whole
group.

6. A significant prop can be held by each actor in turn, as
she holds and name her tableau, before passing the
object to the next actor.

7. The actors find a repetitive movement that takes them
out of their tableaux and back into them. This creates a
movement piece that can be featured or used as back
ground to something else.

5. A common thread can be used to unite the piece.

For example: A word or phrase that represents the theme can
be repeated often in different ways. It can be said in canon, in
unison, or by individuals, and used as transitions between
pieces or to punctuate scenes or ideas expressed throughout
the piece.

An object can be present throughout the piece. It can be used
symbolically in various ways, or transformed into whatever
prop is needed at the moment. For example, a large round
parachute, the kind used in children's playground programs,
can be incorporated into a collective. In the opening, all actors

are underneath it. As the lights come up, a chant is heard as they begin to move. Finally, the edges of the chute are picked up by all actors, who wave it as they move in a circle, each with a line to speak related to the theme (the lines come from the writings done after the sharing circle.) The parachute is then used in other contexts throughout the piece. It becomes a cape, a picnic blanket, a curtain to hide a monster from view and so on, until the end of the piece, when the actors again get underneath it as the lights fade to black.

SAMPLE SCRIPT: Excerpt—opening of directed COLLAGE COLLECTIVE

WABADEEN

(phonetic spelling for Arabic word, meaning, "What's Next?")

Actors form a tableau on set made up of two ladders and several boxes and platforms.

JENN: Within me lives a purpose; a reason why I'm here. *(Group echoes "here.")*

INGA: Where? *(Group echoes "where.")*

JENN: And one day soon it will say to me...

Three second beat.

RACHEL: Me, look at me!

LIZ: Hi there, the world needs you. Are you ready?

ADELLE: Me, I'm not some girl who wants that ordinary dream.

CHERYL: If there were ever a time to dare to make a difference, it is now.

LIZ: Not for any grand course, necessarily, but for something that tugs at your heart.

MELISSA: Something that's your dream.

PAUL: Our desires, hopes and dreams can change on the slightest whim.

NICOLE: Or be bred into us forever.

JOEL: We're all looking for something.

JENN: We set goals.

CORINNE: I hope to fulfill my dream.

GORD: I hope to graduate.

NICOLE: I want to lead a healthy life.

INGA: Aren't you healthy now?

ADELLE: I desire to go up in a hot air balloon.

LIZ: I hope to sleep all day.

RACHEL: I desire world peace.

CHERYL: I desire clothes that will fit me.

PAUL: I hope I won't need dentures after all this money on braces.

CORRINE: I hope for an unforgettable journey through life, full of fun, adventures and unbelievable happiness.

DESIRE TABLEAUX with Improvs.

RACHEL *tap dances on top of piano while LIZ plays "dream" song.*

GORD: *(Crosses centre stage, stops.)* Wabadeen. *(Group echoes "wabadeen.")*

RADIO PLAYS

This is a great introduction to script writing without taking the time required to stage the finished product. It also introduces students to another genre that allows for a great deal of creativity, as they are limited only by their imaginations. Plays can be set in any location without regard for staging. Students gain an opportunity to experiment with sounds and voice characterizations.

Method:

1. If available, the class listens to examples of classic radio plays, as well as modern examples. Public libraries and public radio station libraries are a possible source.

2. Genres are discussed. Horror, soap operas (the origin of the term is from radio, where early sponsors of daytime continuing dramas were soap companies), action adventure, cliff-hanger serials, "who done it" (detective), etc.

3. Groups of five or six students are formed, with members of both sexes in each group (for more variety in voice pitches and tones).

4. The requirements of the assignment are handed out and discussed.

5. Each group begins work with brainstorming for genre and story line.

6. Conversations and situations are improvised, and then scripted.

7. Sound effects are planned.

8. Groups rehearse competed plays.

9. Groups are given tape recorders to record their plays.

10. Tapes are played for the whole group to enjoy and offer feedback.

Sample Radio Play assignment:
Requirements:

1. The play should be between five and ten minutes in length.

2. Each actor must play a minimum of two characters. Consider accents and dialects.

3. The play must have a beginning, middle and end (no talk or game shows).

4. The play may contain short commercials, an announcer and station identification breaks (totaling no more than one quarter of the total time).

5. The play must contain a minimum of ten sound effects, from a minimum of six different sources. For example: three sets of footsteps, one door slam, 2 two bells, one horse galloping, one gun shot, two phones ringing. All sound effects must be

made live, not taken from a recorded library of sound effects.

6. The play should be "shot to edit". In other words, recorded in sequence, with no further in-studio editing. If a mistake is made, simply rewind and re-record. This saves on the total project time.

7. The play should be of a recognizable genre.

Evaluation could take the group progress during the creation phases into account, as well as fulfilling the requirements for the finished product. Bonus marks could be given for creativity and voice characterizations.

Variation #1. The play could be written as a cartoon, with all cartoon voices. The characters would vocalize all sound effects. This project would take much less time to put together and is a good alternative if time does not permit a radio play project to be carried out. Students could take their inspiration from a comic script. The ones with animals are the most fun to do. Students must then ask themselves what an owl or chicken would actually sound like and why. They should look at the mouth of an animal to determine how a word would be formed, given for example, that a duck has a bill, but no teeth. Make sure that they are writing their own storyline, putting these characters into a new situation, rather than one from last week's comic page. Discourage them from taking their inspiration from a TV cartoon. They will be tempted to follow an already existing storyline, taking away the creative element of the project and, what's worse, they will try to imitate a voice they have already heard. The project is easiest with students working in pairs, but could also be done in very small groups.

glossary
glos

STAGE POSITIONS

It is possible to work through all of these projects in a very loose, relaxed fashion, without ever making reference to any theatrical terminology. However, if you are actually rehearsing a project for a public performance, it may save time if you are able to say, for example, "Jenny, please cross down stage left," instead of the more time-consuming, "Jenny, could you walk over there a little further left, no, my left, okay, just a bit more. Okay, now just go towards the front a little more. No, front is towards me." You get the picture.

Although we will talk about a typical rectangular shaped stage, any stage can be divided into areas like a grid so that everyone can learn the names of the areas and identify them instantly.

The front of the stage nearest the audience is called downstage. In the early days of theatre, rather than have the audience on raised seating, the stage itself was tilted, or raked, towards the audience, so they would be able to see what was going on at the back of the stage, or upstage area. The sides of the stage are labeled according to the actor's right and left, not the director's. On a large stage, the positions would look like this:

UR	UCR	UC	UCL	UL
R	CR	C	CL	L
DR	DCR	DC	DCL	DL

LEGEND:

C = Centre
L = Left
R = Right
D = Down
U = Up

These are abbreviations of the terms. Each of them could also have the word Stage in the middle, as in, DL = DSL, (downstage left) and L, could be expressed as SL (stage left).

If the stage is so small as to make the labeling a little ridiculous, as each area would be about one square foot, the centre left and centre right areas can be eliminated, leaving only nine stage areas in total.

UR	UC	UL
R	C	L
DR	DC	DL

LEGEND:

C = Centre
L = Left
R = Right
D = Down
U = Up

STAGE AND ACTING TERMINOLOGY

There are many terms that are used in the theatre that may be unfamiliar to anyone who has not been exposed to them. Some of the more common terms are as follows:

Ad-lib: To improvise action or dialogue within a scene.

Apron: The portion of the stage that lies in front of the curtain.

Auditorium: The part of the theatre that seats the audience.

Backstage: The areas of the stage that are not seen by the audience.

Blocking:
1. The collective movements of the actors in the play as a whole.
2. Obstructing the audience's view of something on the stage.

Border: A short length of curtain hung across the stage, above the playing area, to mask the loft from the audience's view.

Countercross: A shifting of position by one actor, when another actor crosses his path, done to minimize the amount of time the front actor is blocking the actor behind her. Or, the shifting of more than one actor in order to balance the stage picture.

Cue: The last words of a dialogue or an action of one actor that signals the action or dialogue of another actor, or a technical change in sound or lighting.

Cyc or cyclorama: A background curtain around the back of the playing area on stage. It could be black, to mask the backstage area, or white, to be coloured by the lighting.

Drop: A length of fabric, usually canvas, hung from the grid, attached top and bottom to battens.

Exit or exeunt: The word for leaving the stage.

Flat: A wooden frame covered with canvas fabric and used a backdrop in a box set.

Flies or loft: The area above the stage where scenery is hung, masked from the audience.

Fly: To lower and raise scenery to the stage level.

Gauze or scrim: A large curtain, make of heavy gauze fabric, which is semi-transparent when backlit and opaque when lit from the front.

Gibberish: A made-up language. Sounds resembling a specific language.

Give focus: To direct the audience's gaze either by stage position or lighting, or to give focus to a specific actor by the gaze of other actors on stage.

Green room: A backstage room for the actors to lounge in or wait for entrances.

Legs: Lengths of cloth hung on each side of the stage to mask the backstage area.

Monologue: A speech said by one character.

Motivated movement: Any movement by a character that has a reason or motivation.

Places: The call for actors and crew to find their opening positions for the start of a show.

Proscenium: The arch enclosing a stage. The opening between the stage and the auditorium.

Sight line: An imaginary line drawn from a position on the stage to the corner of the auditorium to define the portion of the stage visible to audiences seated at the sides of the theatre.

Stage cross or cross: Any movement of an actor from one area of the stage to another.

Stage picture: What the audience sees on the stage. The positions of the actors.

Strike: The call from the stage manager to remove set pieces from the stage, or to remove the entire set.

Traveller: A front curtain having a centre opening and moving to the left and right, rather than up and down.

Two-hander: A scene with two characters.

Upstaging: To steal focus or attention from another actor at an inappropriate time. This can be done in a variety of ways:

- Making noises, faces (mugging), or performing actions while others should have focus.

- Standing upstage of an actor during a two-way dialogue, thereby forcing him to turn upstage in order to continue the conversation. His back is now presented to the audience and he is giving focus to the upstage actor, directing the audience's gaze there as well.

Wings: The backstage areas on the right and left of the playing area. Also, the curtains or flats masking the stage right and left sides, providing the stage with side entrances.

appendix
app

STRUCTURING

In structuring a beginning level drama lesson, you need first to identify what your goals and objectives are. These might vary considerably, depending on the circumstances of the lesson. For example, it might be part of a long-term course, a one-time master class or workshop or part of a larger structure, with drama adding a small component. Whatever the structure, the class is likely to have these objectives in common:

■ allow students to feel safe and comfortable

■ introduce students to basic drama/acting skills

■ Increase the students' level of self-confidence and creativity

Of course, the aim is also to have them feel energized and interested in the material being presented.

There are exercises that will do all of these things, in a non-threatening manner that's fun for everyone. The following structural suggestions are made for varying lengths of classes. They are examples only. The order of the types of exercises isn't so important. What is important is that the structure is varied, so that students don't become bored by spending a long time in a certain configuration. For example: spending the entire class in a circle, or the entire class with the same partner. Mix up the configurations to provide a fuller experience. As long as the class begins with a warm-up and doesn't do anything with a performance component until they are ready for it, there are any number of ways to put things together. It is possible to begin with individual warm-ups and move to group warm-ups, or the other way around. The following examples have a specific skill as their theme; the warm-up exercises would compliment that theme.

A LESSON

Structure for a 30- to 40-minute lesson:

1. Group warm-up—spread out.
2. Group warm-up—circle.
3. Partner warm-up.
4. Individual warm-up, or, trust, concentration, stupid trick or relaxation exercise
5. Skill exercise—pantomime, tableaux, voice, improv or creating a character.
6. Group performance exercise.

Sample: Introduction to pantomime: beginning level

1. Atom 2	5 minutes
2. Pass the ball	5 minutes
3. Back to back	5 minutes
4. Individual pantomime	5 minutes
5. Board game	5-10 minutes
6. Moved by an object	5-10 minutes

Structure for a 55- to 75-minute lesson:

1. Group warm-up—spread out
2. Group warm-up—circle
3. Partner warm-up
4. Individual warm-up
5. Trust, concentration, stupid trick or relaxation exercise
6. Skill exercises—pantomime, tableaux, voice, improv or creating a character
7. Group performance exercise

Sample: Introduction to Improv: beginning level

1. Take a move	5 minutes
2. Transform an object	5-10 minutes
3. Don't drop the toothpick	5 minutes
4. What is it?	5 minutes

5. Trucks	10 minutes
6. Improv rules	5 minutes
Let's	5 minutes
Give a gift	5-10 minutes
7. The body	10-15 minutes

A WORKSHOP

Structure for an hour- and-a-half to two-hour lesson:

1. Group warm-up—spread out.
2. Group warm-up—circle.
3. Partner warm-up.
4. Individual warm-up.
5. Trust, concentration, stupid trick or relaxation exercise.
6. Small Group Warm-up.
7. Partner Improv.
8. Skill exercises—pantomime, tableaux, voice, improv or creating a character.
9. Group performance exercise.

Sample: Creating a Character: Advanced level

1. Hello	5 minutes
2. Join in with a Who	5-10 minutes
3. Out of Danger	5-10 minutes
4. Where am I?	5 minutes
5. Speech in a Minute (in character)	20 minutes
6. You're famous	10-15 minutes
7. Pick an "A"	10-15 minutes
8. Like an Animal	20-30 minutes
9. Common Location	10-15 minutes

Structure for a short unit or workshop: Theme—Status

The objective is to take students through a progression of exercises that will introduce them to the concept of status and teach them how to use it in character development. This can then be applied to writing monologues, scenes and in any character analysis work.

Exercise progression:

- Hypnotic Trance
- The Party
- The Empire
- One Up
- Get higher
- Switch Status—pairs
- Switch Status—audience
- Ranking
- Find a Friend
- Pulling Faces
- Character analysis of scripted work—
  play suitable for the age level
- Students write own scenes, based on improvs or real life

In the same way, exercises can be pulled from various chapters and linked together to form a unit based on a theme. This might be a skill-based theme, such as pantomime, or any other theme, such as war or love, with all exercises using that theme. The theme will dictate the situations given for improvisations and group performance exercises.

A UNIT

Structure for a Unit Plan: Introduction to drama, non-specific theme

Example: Ten one-hour lessons

Lesson #1
Name Game
Group, individual and partner warm-ups
Low Organized Game
Improv introduction
Group performance exercise

Lesson #2
Warm-ups
Trust exercise
Improv—pairs
Tableaux introduction
Group performance exercise

Lesson #3
Warm-ups
Relaxation exercise
Improv—pairs
Pantomime introduction
Group performance exercise

Lesson #4
Warm-ups
Stupid Trick
Improv—pairs
Creating a Character introduction
Group performance exercise

Lesson #5
Warm-ups
Concentration exercise
Improv—pairs
Status introduction
Group Performance exercise

Lesson #6
Warm-ups
Pair improvs
Group improv—tag team
Improv with Audience

Lesson #7
Warm-ups
Voice exercises
Limericks/poetry
Improv—pairs
Improv with audience

Lesson #8
Warm-ups
Voice exercises
*Reader's Theatre introduction
        Assign groups
        Chose themes

Lesson #9
Warm-ups (brief)
Voice exercises
Reader's Theatre rehearsal time

Lesson #10
Warm-up (brief)
Voice exercises
Reader's Theatre
        Last run-through in groups
        Performance
        Group discussion—critique of all pieces

*Reader's Theatre is acting as a final group project for this mini-course structure. Fairytale Theatre, a Collage Collective, Ancient Ritual or Creating a Character leading to a monologue would also work. This is somewhat dependent on the age of the participants.

Example: Young children, ages five to eight—no group project—leader leads exercises until the end of the course. Story theatre could be done in groups, but with the leader directing each stage with groups working simultaneously. Using nursery rhymes may work better with five-year-olds, as they are shorter.
        Middle years, ages nine to twelve—Fairy Tale Theatre or Reader's Theatre.
        Teens—Fairytale Theatre—with a short story suitable for the group. Reader's Theatre, Ancient ritual, Character monologues or a Collage Collective.
        Adult—Reader's Theater, Collage Collective or Character Monologues

A COURSE

Structure for a full school year course:

- Weeks one and two—introductory name games, warm-ups and simple group performance exercises.

- Weeks three and four—add concentration, trust and introductory pair improv exercises.

- Second month—still lots of warm-up exercises, concentration, stupid tricks, tableaux, etc. and pair improvs, with group performance exercises to end the classes.

- Third month—add voice exercises, group improv exercises like, Join in with a Who and tag team improv.

- Fourth month—add some improv with an audience, if the group seems ready for it, but still keep the emphasis on total group involvement at most times.

- Fifth month—begin to alternate units of small group projects with leader-centred teaching units. Example: Story-telling legends—three or four classes from group formation to performance, followed by four or five classes of improv training.

- Sixth month—unit on Music, mime and tableaux, leading into group project on Ancient rituals.

- Seventh month—unit (five to ten classes) on skill unit of leader's choice (mime, stage fighting, if leader is comfortable with teaching it,) or a unit on status, and a small group project such as Reader's Theatre.

- Eight month—Unit on Creating a Character, leading into a unit on writing and performing a monologue.

- Ninth month—unit on voice production and poetry, leading into small group project on radio or cartoon plays

- Tenth month—teach stage terms, followed by final group project. Example — Fairytales performed for young audience or Collage Collective performed for an audience of peers.

bibliography
SELECTED

bibliography
SELECTED

Booth, David and Charles Lundy, *Improvisation: Learning Through Drama*, Toronto: Academic Press Canada, 1985

Grasham and Gooder, *Improving Your Speech*, New York: Harcourt, Brace and World, Inc., 1960.

Hohenstein, Mary, *A Compact Encyclopedia of Games, Games, Games for People of All Ages*, Minneapolis: Bethany House Publishers, 1980.

Kemp, David, *A Different Drummer: An Ideas Book for Drama*, Toronto: McClelland and Stewart, 1972.

McCaslin, Nellie, *Creative Drama in the Classroom and Beyond*, 7th ed., New York: Longman, 1999.

Polsky, Milton, *Let's Improvise*, Englewood Cliffs, NJ: Prentice-Hall, 1980.

Spolin, Viola, *Improvisation for the Theatre*, Evanston, IL: Northwest University Press, 1963.